Living the Beatitudes

See How You Are Being Conformed to the Image of Christ

By John W. Fogal, Sr.

Published by ChurchSmart Resources

We are an evangelical Christian publisher committed to producing excellent products at affordable prices to help church leaders accomplish effective ministry in the areas of church planting, church growth, church renewal and leadership development.

All Scripture quoted is New International Version unless otherwise noted. The punctuation and capitalizations from each translation are being maintained.

For a free catalog of our resources call 1-800-253-4276.
Visit us at **www.ChurchSmart.com**

Cover design by: Julie Becker
Edited by: Laura Tarro

Copyright © 2013

ISBN: 978-1-936812-02-8

Contents

Preface

Health and being healthy are hot topics. Experts predict that before long our federal government will be spending 20 percent of its budget on healthcare. All kinds of mental disorders continue to plague our society. Social ills and dysfunction scream for attention in our media headlines and TV shows. But the greatest need of all is spiritual health.

Since 1999, I've had the privilege of being involved in a ministry of helping churches become healthier. I have used the Natural Church Development survey tool more than 250 times to assess the current health of churches and then to coach each church through a process of becoming healthier. When a church repeated the survey, 85 percent of the time the health scores improved significantly and, on average, the attendance grew by 20 percent.

I am still very passionate about church health. I don't see it as a mere fad but as another way to understand revival. A revived church is a healthy church, and a healthy church is a revived church. But I am equally concerned about personal spiritual health. I don't see a dichotomy between church health and individual spiritual health. Personal spiritual health (including that of the leaders) is to be developed and maintained in the context of a healthy, vibrant, local expression of the body of Christ—not in isolation.

I have become convinced that church health cannot be sustained if individual members are not spiritually healthy—as is true with our physical bodies. (We are not physically healthy if even one part of our body is full of disease.) Therefore, we must also focus on the spiritual health of each member of the body of Christ. We have learned some things about what a healthy church looks like, but *what does a spiritually healthy individual look like*? The goal of this book is to answer that question and show that "Christ in you" is the only way to become spiritually healthy.

The basic proposition of this book is that God's purpose for every person is "to be conformed to the likeness of His Son" (Romans 8:29). That likeness is often vague and nebulous in the minds of people and needs some tangible, concrete terms to help clarify the concept. Jesus described this likeness by giving us an eight-sided picture of Himself in what we call the "BE-attitudes." And people living those Beatitudes in the life of a local church are spiritually healthy.

As I understand the Bible, there have been only three people who ever lived on planet earth that experienced perfect personal spiritual health—Adam and Eve (before the fall) and Jesus Christ, who "left us an example that we should follow." Adam and Eve were made in the image of God and then sinned—which utterly marred that image. Jesus did not come to take on the image of man. He "took on flesh" and "showed us the Father" because "He is the image of the invisible God" in bodily form. As we study the life of Christ, we see what personal spiritual health looks like. Since Jesus was the kind of preacher who not only practiced what He preached but preached what He practiced, we have in the Beatitudes a snapshot of what personal spiritual health looks like.

As we study each Beatitude, we will see how Jesus modeled that attitude for us. We will also see how each Beatitude is to be lived in the life of a local church and in everyday life. My prayer is that reading this book will be an edifying experience for you and result in your becoming more and more like the Master. Can you imagine being part of a local church where the majority of members are living the Beatitudes?

I can, because I've experienced just enough to want more.

Acknowledgments

The journey of this book began over forty years ago in the Fulton Alliance Church, in Fulton, New York. I had recently become the pastor and sensed the need of a framework for the life and ministry of that church. I believe it was God who led me to preach a series of messages on the Beatitudes. The results were:

- My attitude toward the Christian life and ministry were radically changed.
- The attitudes of a significant number of people in the church, especially the influencers, were radically changed.
- An effective counseling ministry based on the Beatitudes was established.
- Classic church problems were averted.
- The church became a healthier, growing, reproducing church.

The journey continued with two more series of messages on the Beatitudes in that church with new insights and responses; the privilege of sharing these truths with missionaries during their annual conferences in Hong Kong; the Philippines; Japan; Burkina Faso and Mali, Africa. The trail also went to adult classes in the Westview Alliance Church and The Chapel in Fort Wayne, Indiana, and the First Alliance Church and the Monday night Bible study at Citrus Woods Estates in Lakeland, Florida. There were also a number of stops along the way in small-group Bible studies, with each of these opportunities providing excellent feedback.

Along the way, I've studied a number of books written by godly scholars. (See the "For Further Reading" list in the back of the book.) These authors have fed my spiritual life, not just given me intellectual stimulation. I know there must have been truths that I read in their books that have become an integral part of my thought patterns, and have found their way into this manuscript, but now I can't tell you where I got them. However, I acknowledge that "there is nothing new under the sun," and I am indebted to those who have blazed the trail ahead of me.

As I began to write, Dr. Brad Burke, the Rev. Craig Hofer, the Rev. Terry Smith, and Mr. Ray Treen read the chapters and graciously gave me valuable feedback. The Rev. Gary Endersby, Mr. Michael Motter, and Mr. Harold Palmer met with me thirteen Thursday mornings for one hour to discuss a chapter and give me their input. Mike used these chapters as the basis for a weekly men's Bible study that he led; their contributions are in this book. I am so grateful for all their help.

One evening while Bob and Linda Hall were visiting in our home, Linda volunteered to edit the manuscript. What a blessing! I can't imagine anyone's wanting to edit (which shows you how much I need an editor), but Linda just loves doing it. She is gracious, diligent, meticulous, thorough, and does the work of an editor with expertise and excellence. I wish I knew how many times I read Linda's (and all the others') suggestions and said to myself, Why didn't I say it that way? One disclaimer: if you find a typo or some inconsistent grammar or punctuation, it came about after Linda finished her fourth round of editing.

David Wetzler, the founder and owner of ChurchSmart Resources is one of the most godly and generous entrepreneurs I know. He has been a great encouragement to me over the past fifteen years in the ministry of helping churches become healthier and now in the writing of this book. Those who work with him: Laura Tarro, editor and Julie Becker, designer of the cover, have worked diligently and, with their expertise, they have complemented the content of these pages.

Over the years, a few people have said a few (very few) nice things about my writing, but none have ever used the word "eloquent." I take full responsibility for the content, but if you see any hint of literary art, it comes from the people named above. One of my fears in writing a book is that an hour after I hit "send" for the last time, I will have a thought that won't get in the manuscript. These people have minimized that possibility, and I'm extremely grateful.

When you undertake a project like this, you realize you are not doing it alone. I am grateful to God for the godly influence of parents, pastors, Sunday school teachers, Bible college professors, radio and conference speakers, close friends, and mentors who have impacted my life. I look back over so many "intersections" where the paths of others have crisscrossed my journey, and I'm the better for them. The most recent relationship happened when Les Middleton, a man with extensive past experience in and a deep passion for publishing, moved two doors from us at just the right time and became a dear friend. All those "tributaries" have contributed to this book, and I express my gratitude.

I have reserved the expression of my deepest gratitude for my wife, Bonnie. Without her, this book would never have been written. She has been a constant encouragement at my side. She did her proofreading before anyone else saw the manuscript; nobody could have done it better. She had to put up with my mind being consumed with this book for many months, yet she never complained. Thank you, honey, for your faithful love and support.

Ultimately, I thank God for His working in my life, enabling me to see truth and write this book. I reflect on the many times when I was writing or reading what I had written and was deeply moved as I realized what God was doing. So many times I've been amazed at the meshing of events and internal impressions which have ended up on the pages of this book. My prayer is that, as you read, you will praise God for what you read and for the way His truth feeds your spiritual life!

1

Setting the Stage

Now when he saw the crowds, he went up on a mountainside and sat down.
His disciples came to him, and he began to teach them. (Matthew 5:1-2)

The phrase "The Sermon on the Mount" is not in the Bible. According to church historians, this title was first used by Augustine when he wrote his commentary on the gospel of Matthew in the fourth century. In this sermon, Jesus gives us the essence of life in His new kingdom. The Beatitudes, at the beginning of the sermon, give us a portrait of the ideal citizen in His kingdom. These are some of the best-known teachings of Jesus; the epitome of His oral ministry on earth; the most often quoted and among the most remarkable pronouncements He ever made. So, let's look at the setting and the brief introduction that Matthew gives for this great sermon.

THE PREPARATION

If we read only Matthew's account of the life and ministry of Christ, we get the impression that only a few events happened before Jesus gave the major discourse we call the Sermon on the Mount. The chronology appears to be that Jesus "was about thirty years old" (Luke 3:23) when the following happened:

- He was baptized by John the Baptist in the Jordan River.
- He was led by the Spirit into the desert where He fasted for 40 days and was tempted by the devil.
- He began to preach, "Repent, for the kingdom of heaven is near."
- He called four of His disciples to follow Him.
- He healed the sick, and large crowds followed Him.
- He saw the crowds and preached the Sermon on the Mount.

However, when we read *The NIV Harmony of the Gospels*, it seems clear that many more events took place before the Sermon on the Mount was preached. It seems that most of the biblical scholars who try to harmonize the Gospel records in chronological order do so by starting with Luke's account, probably the last of the synoptic Gospels to be written. Dr. Luke—a physician and historian—writes, "Since I myself have carefully investigated everything from the beginning, it seemed good also to me to write an orderly account for you, most excellent Theophilus" (Luke 1:3). So, it would make sense to use Luke's chronology as a starting point and fit the other accounts into his "carefully investigated . . . orderly account." When we do that, we find some "gaps" in Matthew's account in chapter four between verses 11 . . . 12 . . . 13-16 . . . 17-22 . . . 23-25. The composite picture of this time period includes: Jesus' teaching on many occasions; Jesus' performing many miracles that declared His deity; Jesus' facing issues regarding the Sabbath and His equality with the Father; Jesus' choosing other disciples such as Matthew. A careful reading of the Gospels reveals that by this time, He had many disciples ("who were with Him") and thousands of followers. Think of the opportunities for preparation Jesus had with a large number of disciples before He chose the twelve apostles from among them.

Preparation is a very significant concept. I am writing this as we are coming up to the Super Bowl. Think of the years of preparation that each player and the two teams experienced. Then think about all the buildup of preparation during the two weeks prior to the game. Think about the preparation for a book like this. I first preached a series of messages on the Beatitudes more than forty years ago. As you read in the "acknowledgments," there have been many times of preparation since then—each with new insights and applications. Now, in these past months, there has been a crescendo in the preparation.

So it was with the coming of Christ and His ministry on earth. In the grand scheme of God's timing, preparation really began in eternity past, since He was the "Lamb that was slain from the creation of the world" (Revelation 13:8). Think of all the prophetic statements in the Old Testament that filled God's people with hope as they anticipated the coming of the Messiah. God called and prepared John the Baptist to "prepare the way of the Lord." After His public introduction by John, Jesus was led by the Holy Spirit into the desert where He was prepared by prayer and fasting and temptation by the devil. His ministry began slowly, with no fanfare. He built up a reputation that preceded Him wherever He went, so He could preach what He was already practicing.

By the time Jesus arrived at this mountainside, which some say was probably more than two years into His public ministry, great crowds were following Him. He had "spent the night praying to God. When morning came, he called his disciples to him and chose twelve of them, whom he also designated apostles" (Luke 6:12-13). Most people casually assume that the twelve were designated as apostles from the beginning of His earthly ministry, but there was deliberate preparation before He chose them. After all this preparation, Jesus gives what could be called an "ordination charge" to His leadership team.

THE PLACE

The Sermon on the Mount was preached on a mountainside. Tradition has it at a spot located on a level place on the side of a hill overlooking the north end of the Sea of Galilee designated as the "Mount of Beatitudes."

Many mountains (or "mounts") are highlighted in the Bible as places of encounter with God and sites of unusual spiritual experiences. After the epic flood, the ark rested on *Mount Ararat* and there God revealed Himself to Noah and his family. It was to *Mount Moriah* that Abraham went to sacrifice his son Isaac and where God provided a ram instead. *Mount Sinai* was where God met with Moses and gave him the Ten Commandments written by "the finger of God." *Mount Zion* is where King David built the "city of David" and where the King of kings will reign during His millennial kingdom. Elijah challenged the prophets of Baal on *Mount Carmel* and there God sent fire from heaven. Mountains provided a special refuge for Jesus as He spent time alone with His Father in prayer. The *Mount of Transfiguration* certainly was a mountaintop experience for those three disciples—Peter, James, and John. Outside of the city of Jerusalem is the *Mount of Olives* where Jesus often taught His disciples. This is the same mount from which He ascended to heaven and where He will "set His foot" when He returns. Appropriately, the *Mount of Beatitudes*, where Jesus preached this sermon, is in the same category of extraordinary places. Seeing this fact places the Beatitudes on a par with the Ten Commandments, for example, in significance.

THE PREACHER

We can learn a lot about a person just by listening to him or her speak. In giving us the Beatitudes, Christ allowed us to see deeply into His nature and know who He really is. Sadly, some preachers don't practice what they preach. Others try to practice what they preach. But Jesus preached what He practiced and revealed how He thought.

The text in Matthew 5:1 says that Jesus "sat down," not because He was weary, but because that was the customary teaching posture for a Jewish rabbi in those days. He often stood when He preached, but since this was an official discourse He spoke ex cathedra ("from the chair").

The text also says Jesus "opened His mouth" although, for some reason, this is not included in the NIV. Certainly we can teach without opening our mouths. In fact, some communication is best done without words. There are times when what we do speaks so loudly that people don't hear what we say. More things are caught than taught. But, "opened His mouth" is significant as a Greek expression for a solemn discourse when a person is opening his heart and fully pouring out his mind in an intimate, dignified utterance.

"He began to teach them." This means Jesus gave them authoritative instruction. This was not a discussion group where everyone's opinion was of equal value. In just this one sermon Jesus declared six times, "You have heard that it was said to the people long ago . . . but I tell you." That is authority! He spoke from a source beyond Himself. Later on Jesus said, "For I did not speak of my own accord, but the Father who sent me commanded me what to say and how to say it" (John 12:49).

Jesus was an anointed preacher. He was "full of the Holy Spirit" (Luke 4:1). He had "the Spirit without limit" (John 3:34). When Jesus preached in the synagogue in Nazareth, He said, "The Spirit of the Lord is on me, because he has anointed me to preach good news to the poor" (Luke 4:18). This made Him a very powerful and effective preacher. At the end of this sermon, "the crowds were amazed at his teaching, because he taught as one who had authority, and not as their teachers of the law" (Matthew 7:28-29). Earlier, Jesus had a conversation with a Samaritan woman at the well; revival broke out in her home town of Sychar where "because of his words many more became believers" (John 4:41). Later, even the temple guards said, "No one ever spoke the way this man does" (John 7:46). The people were spellbound by this itinerant preacher, and thousands followed Him to hear His next words.

> APPLICATION: Those who preach the Word of God must preach what they receive from God and preach what they practice "with a demonstration of the Spirit's power, so that your faith might not rest on men's wisdom, but on God's power" (1 Corinthians 2:4-5).

THE PEOPLE

Who was in the audience that day? Was it the crowd? Was it the disciples? I believe it was both. Jesus had just chosen the twelve apostles, and "He went down with them and stood on a level place" (Luke 6:17). So, the twelve apostles were there. But, the narrative goes on to say, "A large crowd of his disciples was there and a great number of people from all over Judea, from Jerusalem, and from the coasts of Tyre and Sidon, who had come to hear him and to be healed of their diseases" (Luke 6:17-18).

Picture this in your mind. The church is in the world with people of the world on the outside looking in. But, in the church, there are circles within circles. In Jesus' day (before the 3000 were added on the day of Pentecost) there was a circle of more than 500 people to whom Jesus appeared "at the same time" after His resurrection and before His ascension (1 Corinthians 15:6). Then there was the circle of 120 in the upper room (Acts 1:15). Next there was a circle of 70 disciples (or 72, depending on which translation you read) sent out "two by two" by Jesus (Luke 10:1). We've already seen the next circle of twelve apostles chosen by Christ. In a number of places we see an inner circle of three—Peter, James, and John. And, finally, there was the one "disciple [John] whom Jesus loved" (John 13:23). I believe that all these circles of people, as well as those outside these circles, were represented in the crowd that day.

The more intriguing question is who was in the target audience in the mind of Christ as He spoke that day? I believe it was the disciples which includes the twelve apostles and the "large crowd of His disciples." Matthew 5:1-2 says, "His disciples came to him, and he began to teach them." The crowd in the outer circle was sort of a secondary audience. This same scenario happened in the Corinthian church when they were meeting for worship and "some unbelievers come in" (1 Corinthians 14:23-24). This sermon is not directed toward everyone; it is for believers. The Beatitudes are practically meaningless to the person who has never trusted Jesus Christ as Savior (1 Corinthians 1:18). Jesus is not teaching unbelievers that they need to live this way in order to become Christians. They need to be saved in order to live this way. If you are in His kingdom and Christ is your King, then these should be your basic attitudes.

> APPLICATION: The Sermon on the Mount does not apply to nations, but to individuals. All (nations and every individual) are under God's sovereign rule and are to obey biblical principles. But "turning the other cheek" is for individuals, not the judicial system. A spirit of revenge is never right, but government leaders are morally and ethically responsible for punishing evil.

Many see the Beatitudes as a beautiful, idealistic, ethical treatise, but impossible to practice. Later, Jesus made it even more difficult when He said, "Be perfect, therefore, as your heavenly Father is perfect" (Matthew 5:48). This mandate causes some to put off the application of these truths until the millennial kingdom. However, Jesus had already been preaching that "the kingdom of heaven is near"—now, imminent, present

(Matthew 4:17). He also promised persecution and taught us how to respond appropriately, but there is no scriptural evidence of persecution in the millennial kingdom. In addition, these same principles are taught in the Epistles for the church to live out in this present age.

Others go to the opposite extreme and dilute this teaching down to the level of human attainment—and, in so doing, deny the authority of Scripture and the work of the Holy Spirit in our lives. God wants to give us a new nature and provide for us, by His grace, all that we need for life and godliness here and now.

THE PRONOUNCEMENT

"Blessed are . . ." says volumes. First, let's think about what it is *not*.

Blessedness is* not *about fleeting externals. It is not found in the acquisition of earthly possessions. Jesus made it clear: "A man's life does not consist in the abundance of his possessions" (Luke 12:15). Solomon had wealth, power, prestige, and women, but these things did not bring blessedness. His conclusion was: "all is vanity." The word "blessed" is used over fifty times in the New Testament but never refers to short-lived prosperity.

Blessedness is* not *happiness as the world sees happiness. "Happiness" comes from an old-English word meaning "happenings." For most people happiness is an emotion that depends on what is happening around them at the moment. People instinctively want happiness. In America we see happiness as an inalienable right to pursue as given to us by our Creator. Joy, on the other hand, is an enduring quality because it comes from deep within our soul and is not affected by the circumstances surrounding us. It is not possible to always be happy. It is possible to always have the joy of the Lord. However, happiness and joy can be used synonymously in Scripture, and in real life it is sometimes difficult to distinguish between the two. For example: at a wedding, do you feel happy or joyful or both? We need to be careful not to think of happiness as something that only worldly-minded people experience and joy as only for heaven-bound saints.

The word "blessed" comes from a Greek word basically meaning "happy" or "blissful." I like David Jeremiah's title for his book on the Beatitudes—*How to be Happy According to Jesus*. Just remember what Jesus said, "Happy are the poor . . . happy are the mourners . . . happy are the hungry . . . happy are the persecuted." He is saying that happy people are people who have the right attitudes.

"Blessed are . . ."* is not *some common, often repeated, everyday cliché like politicians ending their speeches by saying "God Bless America"; like people glibly saying "God bless you" when someone sneezes; or like saying the "blessing" at mealtime.

Second, let's think about what "blessed" *is*.

It is an adjective used to describe the character of God Himself. Psalm 68:35 says, "Blessed be God" (ASV); Psalm 72:18, "Blessed be the Lord God" (ASV); Psalm 119:12, "Blessed art Thou, O Lord" (ASV). In 1 Timothy 1:11, Paul writes about the "blessed God" and in 1 Timothy 6:15, he calls God "the blessed and only Ruler, the King of kings and Lord of lords." So God is by nature blessed, fulfilled, satisfied, blissful, and happy. That is a description of the divine nature. Peter declares that we as believers "become partakers of the divine nature" (2 Peter 1:4 ASV). God wants us to be blessed, fulfilled, satisfied, blissful, and happy, and He makes that possible through the new birth.

"Blessedness" is a glorious, overflowing, exuberant, ecstatically joyful exclamation—"Oh, the blessedness of . . .!" (Note the exclamation point.) I am fond of Max Lucado's title for his book on the Beatitudes, *The Applause of Heaven.* "Blessed" means to be supremely happy, to be spiritually prosperous, to be divinely favored, to be delightfully contented, and to have God's approval. It is the ultimate well-being and distinctive spiritual joy of those who share in the life of Christ. It is the joyous thrill of victory over sin and the devil and the radiant gladness of the Christian life. "Blessed" is a word full of sunshine. It is God's benediction upon us. The people to whom Christ makes this pronouncement are to be congratulated—without any sense of pride, because this is all by God's amazing grace.

To most people this understanding of "blessedness" does not make sense. They think that happiness is about—
- Being prosperous and wealthy, not "poor in spirit."
- Laughing, living the dream, and never suffering from misery and pain.
- Being self-assertive pushers, demanding what they want when they want it.
- Being self-sufficient, not needing anything from anyone else.
- Having people at their mercy rather than reaching out to people in need.
- Dulling the conscience so they can enjoy doing what is wrong.
- Being self-centered troublemakers so people notice them.
- Certainly not smiling when being ill-treated.

"Blessedness" is spiritual and internal, completely independent of outside circumstances. This blessedness is real and lasting—a happy, contented condition of the soul that is eternal. It is so unusual, so penetrating, that it requires a complete paradigm shift, a whole new set of core values. Jesus turned everything upside down. He starts on the inside and works out. The spiritual comes first. Example: "Praise be to the God and Father of our Lord Jesus Christ, who has blessed us in the heavenly realms with every spiritual blessing in Christ" (Ephesians 1:3). "Blessed is the man whose sin the LORD does not count against him" (Psalm 32:2). Wow! Forgiven—no remorse, no condemnation, no punishment in hell forever, a clean heart, and a clear conscience—that is being blessed!

APPLICATION: Let's never "dumb down" the glorious inheritance that is ours as believers in Jesus Christ, thus making Christianity just one among many religions. And let's never forget that we are "saved by grace"!

THE PURPOSE

If we were to ask a hundred people, "What is Jesus like?" we would get many different answers. The responses would be largely dependent upon what they were taught (or not taught) in Sunday school or the pictures of Jesus they may have seen over the years. One person may describe Him as a person who "went about doing good." Another individual may see Him as a victim hanging on a cross. Still another would remember the story of Jesus with a whip, driving the moneychangers out of the temple. Others would picture Him as the gentle shepherd with a little lamb in His arms. Some would see Him as a great teacher, while still others would see Him as a carpenter's son. Some might recall His scathing rebukes to the Pharisees, while others would describe the scene of Him with a little child on His knee. A few might think of Him as a servant washing the disciples' feet, while others will feel challenged by the Great Commission He gave us with "all authority in heaven and on earth" (Matthew 28:18).

Each of these mental pictures (and many more) taken in isolation could easily become distorted images of the Son of God because they are one-dimensional views. How can we have a true, balanced, biblical understanding of what Jesus is really like in all of His complexity and uniqueness? Certainly, reading the Gospel accounts of the life of Christ will give us a many-sided picture of the God-Man. But I believe that Christ gave us an introductory, outlined revelation of who He really is on the inside when He spoke the Beatitudes.

One purpose of the Beatitudes was to give us a portrait of the preacher Himself. He is preaching what He practiced (that is quality teaching). In these ten verses we have an eight-sided picture of Christ-likeness. This multi-faceted picture is what it looks like to be like Jesus. Each of the next nine chapters in this book will demonstrate how Jesus exemplified a particular Beatitude, with two chapters devoted to the first one.

Some have called this sermon the "Magna Carta of the Kingdom." The history of humankind in the Old Testament begins with God making man in His own image. Then sin entered the human race and that image was distorted, polluted, and perverted by the fall. Then, in the New Testament, Christ—who is "the image of the invisible God"—came to show us the Father and, by His atonement and His life in us, He makes it possible for the image of God to be restored in believers. He did not come to take on the image of man. He took on flesh so we could see the image of God in bodily form. Jesus said, "Anyone who has seen me has seen the Father" (John 14:9).

However, for many, *image* is a vague, indefinable word. One of the problems in this study is our fuzziness about what it means to "be conformed to the likeness of his Son" (Romans 8:29). He left us an example "that [we] should follow in his steps" (1 Peter 2:21). But, so often that can easily lead to external actions and legalism. The image of God in Christ was something deeper than what He did.

Here are links in a chain that bring me to my conclusion about the purpose of the Beatitudes:

- Being comes before doing.
- Being and doing flow from our thinking. ("As he thinks in his heart, so is he")
- Thought patterns, a mind-set, and attitudes are all synonyms of "mind."
- We "have the mind of Christ" because of the miraculous impartation of His divine nature by the Holy Spirit.
- That "mind" is revealed in the Beatitudes as Christ preached what He practiced and how He thought.
- The Beatitudes are character qualities that relate to basic thought patterns— BE-attitudes.
- As God works in us, He is fulfilling His purpose in us, which is that we become more and more like His Son.

Since it is true that Jesus is giving us a "Manifesto of the King" as He begins to set up His kingdom; that our thought patterns carve the shape we become; that it is God's purpose to restore in us His image and conform us to the image of His Son; and finally, that Christ came to do the will of His Father, my conclusion is that the purpose of the Beatitudes is to give us an eight-sided composite picture of Christ-likeness. Those who are "in Christ" and "Christ is in them" are to live lives characterized by these qualities.

Related to this, the Beatitudes give us an introductory, outlined snapshot of the mind of Christ. I grew up reading and memorizing verses in the King James Version of the Bible. For me, Philippians 2:5 was "Let this mind be in you, which was also in Christ Jesus." I still remember the day when I first read this verse in the NIV—"Your attitude should be the same as that of Christ Jesus." That started me on a study of "mind" and "attitude." I have come to the conclusion that "having the mind of Christ" is about thought *patterns*, not an isolated thought that darts through our brain. When Jesus rebuked Peter in Mark 8:33, He said, "You do not have in mind the things of God, but the things of men." Paul wrote in Philippians 3:19, "Their mind is on earthly things." You have heard the old adage: "Sow a thought, reap a thought pattern. Sow a thought pattern, reap an action. Sow an action, reap a habit. Sow a habit, reap a character." The key is having the right thought patterns or mind-set, and the right one is the "mind of Christ." Terrorists have a mind-set. Atheists have a mind-set. Ideologues of all kinds have a mind-set. "Baby-boomers" have a mind-set. False teachers have a mind set. Nominal Christians have a mind-set. Fully devoted followers of Christ are to have the mind-set of Christ.

The Bible makes it clear—"as he thinks in his heart, so is he" (Proverbs 23:7 NKJV). Paul writes to the Roman Christians, "Be transformed by the renewing of your mind" (12:2). To the Ephesians he writes, "Be made new in the attitude of your minds; and . . . put on the new self, created to be like God in true righteousness and holiness" (4:23-24). Before we think about "what would Jesus do," we need to think about "what would Jesus think." The goal of this book is to help us reconstruct our thought patterns as we become more and more like the Master. True spirituality is not about having a sanctimonious tone of voice as we pray or a perfect attendance record in Sunday school or keeping all the rules that the legalist requires, etc. It is about having the mind of Christ (1 Corinthians 2:16) as He outlined in the opening statements of the Sermon on the Mount.

The Beatitudes focus our attention on *being* rather than *doing*. Martin Lloyd-Jones says it well, "A Christian is something before he does something." Attitude, as we are using it in this study, refers to an inner state of being related to the pattern of our thinking. So far in my study, I am convinced that everything the Bible teaches about being a Christian can fit under one of these eight headings. While in the first church I had the privilege of pastoring, I preached a message entitled, "The Ninth Beatitude." It was on the subject of gratitude. Now, as you will see in the next chapter, I include it as part of the mind-set of being "poor in spirit." When my wife reads from a devotional book as we spend devotional time together in the mornings, I often say, "Which Beatitude does that come under?" Right now my desk is cluttered with index cards filled with notes for each of these next chapters. These few verses take on more and more significance for me as I continue to study each Beatitude and see the relevance and importance of having the mind of Christ.

Finally, since Christ is giving the previously mentioned ordination charge to His leadership team, He begins with a list of inner qualities that distinguish between those who follow Him and those who don't. He is launching a counterculture based on Christian virtues. Jesus made it clear, "What is highly valued among men is detestable in God's sight" (Luke 16:15). The early church "turned the world upside down" (Acts 17:6 NKJV), which meant it was becoming right side up. The character traits included in the Beatitudes are in bold contrast to the viewpoint of the world. These eight qualities are at the core of Christianity. Their tentacles reach into every area of life. They are becoming more and more counterintuitive as our culture moves further and further away from the Judeo-Christian way of life. Living out the Beatitudes leads to a healthy, balanced, functional, useful, and fruitful life. There is not a more winsome, beautiful life. Therefore, as a believer, I want to know and experience all I can in order to be the kind of person God wants me to be.

THE PARTS OF THE WHOLE

Although each Beatitude is complete in itself and has its own benediction, it is part of the whole picture of Christ-likeness. As we will learn throughout this book, each of these virtues springs out of and rises above what precedes it. Years ago, Jonathan Edwards wrote, "There is a concatenation of the graces of Christianity." *Concatenation* is a word we don't use much anymore, although it is coming back in the world of computers. It means "go together" like the cohesion of water when two streams go together to become one. We see this concept in the life of Christ. He is "very God of very God and very Man of very man." He is "full of grace and truth." He is "the Lion and the Lamb." There are two different realities that come together, even though it may seem to us to be counterintuitive. In the case of the Beatitudes, we also see this idea in the pairing of "happy" with conditions that don't seem to fit—happy are the poor, the mourners, the hungry, the persecuted, etc.

Concatenation also means "to be interdependent." In order for something to be concatenated, there must be two or more things together in an interdependent relationship. Again, as with water, if you have only oxygen or hydrogen, you don't have water. But, if two parts of hydrogen and one part of oxygen are concatenated, you have water. This is how Jonathan Edwards explained why Paul wrote "the fruit of the Spirit is" and not "the fruits of the Spirit are." Thomas Watson, in his book entitled *Beatitudes*, also used concatenation to describe this interaction in the Beatitudes. If only some of the qualities listed in Galatians 5:22 or in the Beatitudes are seen in a person's life, it may be just the natural disposition or temperament of the person. For instance, a person may have a naturally docile temperament leading some to think that that person is really spiritual, when it is only a natural quality that person was born with.

Another reason for experiencing this concatenation is to grow proportionately in all the Christ-like graces. As the beauty of the physical body consists in the symmetry of all the parts in which not only the head grows, but also the arms and torso and legs and so on, so spiritual growth is most beautiful and glorifying to God when there is symmetry and proportion with every Beatitude thriving.

It all starts by entering into a living, spiritual, union relationship with God like the vine and branches described in John 15:1-8 and like the husband-wife relationship, which is vastly different from a friend-with-friend relationship. This is a relationship with God by faith through Christ that begins by acknowledging that I am "poor in spirit." That spiritual bankruptcy is because I was born in sin and I have sinned, which leads to mourning and sorrowing over my sin. My sinfulness causes me to realize that I have no right to assert myself. At this point I begin to have a hunger and thirst for a righteousness that I cannot otherwise have. When I am filled with that righteousness, it manifests itself in mercy, purity, peacemaking, and a willingness to suffer persecution and insult.

However, these Beatitudes cannot be lived only in a sequential, linear mode (from A to B to C). They are to be lived in an interdependent, circular manner (from A to B to C to B to C to A, etc.). As we grow spiritually, we never outgrow the need for the interplay of all these BE-attitudes.

For the one who is "made a new creature in Christ," all of these virtues are strung together and are part of the new life in Christ. When the fruit of the Spirit is seen in a life, there is a concatenation of all the essentials of the Christ-life in us—they go together and are interdependent. Incidentally, this principle is also true of the descriptions of love in 1 Corinthians 13; of the qualifications for elders and deacons in 1 Timothy 3 and Titus 1; of those things we need to "be all the more eager to make your calling and election sure" in 2 Peter 1:5-10.

So, as we study each Beatitude in the following chapters, let's try to understand how they all go together in order to give us a full-orbed picture of Christ-likeness. Then we can say with the songwriter:
> Be like Jesus, this my song,
> In the home and in the throng:
> Be like Jesus all day long!
> I would be like Jesus.

And pray with another songwriter:
> Oh, to be like Thee! Oh, to be like Thee,
> Blessed Redeemer, pure as Thou art!
> Come in Thy sweetness, come in Thy fullness;
> Stamp Thine own image deep on my heart.

PERSONAL-REFLECTION QUESTIONS

- In which circle-within-circles (see page 15 for the description of the concentric circles of Jesus' relationships) are you when it comes to your involvement with Christ and His church?
- How does the idea of "preparation" impact your everyday life?
- How do you deal with the concept of "Be perfect, as your heavenly Father is perfect"?
- What practical implication does "being comes before doing" have in your life?

GROUP-DISCUSSION QUESTIONS

- What are some ways in which we try to "dumb down" Christianity and make it like other religions?
- Who should the "target audience" be when the church is gathered to worship?
- What are some different "mind-sets," and how do they contrast with the mind of Christ?
- What are some commitments/involvements that relate to each of the concentric circles of the church?

2

The Blessedness of Being Poor in Spirit! – Part 1

Blessed are the poor in spirit, for theirs is the kingdom of heaven.
(Matthew 5:3)

Imagine yourself standing with a crowd of people (maybe a thousand or more) on the side of a hill. At the bottom of the hill behind you is the Sea of Galilee and over on the west bank is the little town of Capernaum. In front of you there is a level place where Jesus is seated with His disciples gathered around Him. The crowd presses in to hear what He has to say. You listen. The first words out of His mouth are, "Blessed are the poor in spirit, for theirs is the kingdom of heaven" (Matthew 5:3). How do you think you would have responded?

This seems to be a strange way to begin a sermon. It is contrary to conventional homiletic wisdom and doesn't seem to make a good first impression for most people. Yet, it is not new. The Old Testament is filled with words of encouragement and help for the poor. The psalmist wrote, "This poor man called, and the LORD heard him; he saved him out of all his troubles" (Psalm 34:6). Isaiah wrote that God declares, "This is the one I esteem: he who is humble and contrite in spirit, and trembles at my word" (Isaiah 66:2). Earlier, Jesus said, "The Spirit of the Lord is on me, because he has anointed me to preach good news to the poor" (Luke 4:18).

WHAT DOES "POOR IN SPIRIT" MEAN?

There are at least two words in the Greek language translated "poor." One means having to do manual labor for a living, but when compared with other people, being relatively poor. It implies living below the poverty level. It does not indicate extreme, dire need, but it is the opposite of rich.

The other word (the one used in this verse) means absolute, total, abject poverty. It literally translates to having nothing. It describes a person who is destitute and reduced to begging to keep body and soul together. Someone has described it as—"poverty beaten to its knees." It depicts a beggar after a crust of bread. It is the attitude of the Canaanite woman who came to Jesus as recorded in Matthew 15:21-28 and whose last words in the dialogue were, "Yes, Lord . . . but even the dogs eat the crumbs that fall from their masters' table" (Matthew 15:27). It is poverty so deep that a person must maintain his or her existence by the humiliating activity of begging. Understanding this Beatitude requires a mental picture of the thought patterns of a person in this totally helpless condition.

WHAT DOES "POOR IN SPIRIT" *NOT* MEAN?

It does *not* mean to be "poor spirited"—nasty, miserly, sneaky. Who wants to be like that?

It does *not* mean lack of enthusiasm, the opposite of a "spirited person" who is full of enthusiasm.

It does *not* mean having a poor self-image; going around saying, "Poor me; I'm no good; my parents put me down; my teacher told me that I would never amount to anything. So, let's have a pity party and let me show off my fake humility."

It does *not* mean having a shy, introverted personality as indicated by always being in the background. Some people are born that way and can be proud of that natural temperament.

It is *not* living a self-imposed monastic lifestyle, having taken a "vow of poverty." This type of lifestyle can lead to the worst kind of pride—spiritual pride. God does not pronounce blessing on people because they make themselves poor materially.

It is *not* involuntary financial poverty. Obviously, there is some similarity between the mind-set of a person who is financially poor and a person who is poor in spirit. But the Bible is a poor man's friend. "Has not God chosen those who are poor in the eyes of the world to be rich in faith and to inherit the kingdom he promised those who love him?" (James 2:5). Jesus came down on the side of the poor when He said, "It is easier for a camel to go through the eye of a needle than for a rich man to enter the kingdom of God" (Matthew 19:24). Nevertheless, a person can be:
- Poor financially and rich spiritually;
- Poor financially and still proud, walking with a swagger;
- Rich financially and spiritually impoverished but refusing to acknowledge it;

- Rich financially but with the mind-set of a beggar when it comes to spiritual things.

Let's do a brief history lesson on the subject of pride. According to *Sacred Origins of Profound Things* by Charles Panati, Greek monastic theologian Evagrius of Pontus (AD 345–399) first drew up a list of eight offenses and wicked human passions. Later, Pope Gregory the Great (AD 540–604) combined "vain glory" and "pride" and was the first to give the list the title of "The Seven Deadly Sins." Minor changes have been made since then, but the basic concept remains the same. These early theologians tried to organize different categories or branches of sins from which all sins evolve. They saw pride as the trunk of the tree, the other "deadly sins" as the branches, and the "multitude of sins" as the fruit. Down through the centuries, the sin of pride has been seen as the tap-root for all other sins.

Interestingly, the Bible has its own list of sinful behaviors in Proverbs 6:16-19: "There are six things the LORD hates, seven that are detestable to him: haughty eyes, a lying tongue, hands that shed innocent blood, a heart that devises wicked schemes, feet that are quick to rush into evil, a false witness who pours out lies and a man who stirs up dissension among brothers." It is notable that "pride" or "haughty eyes" head both lists.

In the two lists below, see the contrast between humility and pride. Also, be reminded that this entire discussion is about Christ-likeness vs. evil, life vs. death, heaven vs. hell.

BEATITUDES	SEVEN (originally eight) DEADLY SINS
Being Poor in Spirit	Pride
Being a Mourner	Vain Glory
Being Meek	Envy
Being Hungry & Thirsty for Righteousness	Gluttony
Being Merciful	Anger
Being Pure in Heart	Lust
Being a Peacemaker	Greed
Being Persecuted Because of Righteousness	Sloth

Pride is not just the first in the list of the seven deadly sins; it is the essence of all sins (as being "poor in spirit" is the foundation for all the other basic, Christ-like attitudes). In *Mere Christianity*, C. S. Lewis put it this way: "The essential vice, the utmost evil, is pride. Unchastity, greed, drunkenness, and all that, are mere flea-bites in comparison. Pride leads to every other vice. It is the complete anti-God state of mind." Pride preceded Adam and Eve. Isaiah 14:14 suggests that Lucifer fell because of pride when he said; "I will make myself like the Most High." Adam and Eve yielded to the same temptation when the serpent said, "You will not surely die. . . . For God knows that when you eat of it your eyes will be opened, and you will be like God, knowing good and evil" (Genesis 3:4-5). Pride is the most serious of sins, because it aspires to the status and position of God and refuses to acknowledge our dependency upon God. There is no sin which God hates more than pride. Proverbs 16:5 says, "Everyone proud in heart is an abomination to the LORD . . . none will go unpunished" (NKJV). Isn't it ironic that we as human beings who are so dependent and guilty should be so proud?

The Bible is clear: "God opposes the proud but gives grace to the humble" (James 4:6). The same hand that crushes the proud supports the humble. Isn't it irrational that people think they are resisting God when, in fact, it is God who is resisting those who are proud? Jesus declared, "Whoever exalts himself will be humbled, and whoever humbles himself will be exalted" (Matthew 23:12). He condemned the Pharisees and chief rulers because they wanted the chief seats. The Bible teaches: "Do not be proud," "Do not be conceited," "Do not be puffed up," "Do not think of yourself more highly than you ought to think," "Do not be high-minded."

HUMILITY is the key word for this Beatitude. Humility is a quality that God is looking for and highly esteems. Nobody catches His attention more than those who are genuinely humble and contrite. The Bible exhorts us to "be completely humble" (Ephesians 4:2). Our thought patterns are to be saturated with "humbleness of mind" (Colossians 3:12 KJV). Charles Spurgeon wrote: "Humility is the proper estimate of one's self."

As I have studied this subject, I see humility falling into two main categories:

1. **DEPENDENCE, which is the opposite of INDEPENDENCE and SELF-SUFFICIENCY**
2. **SUBMISSION, which is the opposite of REBELLION and SELF-RULE**

Submission is discussed in the next chapter, but first; let's look at the concept of dependence as part of humility. Again, get the picture in your mind of a beggar who is totally dependent upon others for existence. The beggar is totally helpless in abject poverty. "Poor in spirit" means that we must rely upon God for everything.

Before we begin thinking about the subject of dependence, let's clarify several things. First, we are not talking about a welfare mentality which is the kind of dependence that diminishes personal responsibility. In political circles we hear about "self-reliance" as opposed to "government handouts." That kind of self-reliance is good. The problem comes when we bring that same attitude over to the spiritual realm where we are absolutely incapable of doing anything that is good enough to get us into heaven. Second, this dependence is not in conflict with the goal of parents to have their children become independent by the time they leave home. Maybe that would be better stated as becoming mature enough to fully depend upon God on their own by the time they leave home. Third, this is not about a slavish dependency or co-dependency. It is about a positive, healthy dependence upon God. For example: it is one thing to have a healthy appetite and need food; it is quite another thing to be slavishly dependent upon things such as alcohol or drugs.

Depending upon God is the most normal, healthy, functional, honest, spiritually satisfying thing we can do. Think about how we depend on that which is outside ourselves every day in order to exist. How long would we live without oxygen or water or food? It is in that frame of reference that we acknowledge our dependence upon God when it comes to our spiritual life.

> Depending upon God is the most normal, healthy, functional, honest, spiritually satisfying thing we can do.

The basic question is, "What do you have that you did not receive?" (1 Corinthians 4:7) Nobody is poorer than the person who is unaware of his or her poverty. That was the accusation that Jesus made against the church in Laodicea when He said, "You say, 'I am rich; I have acquired wealth and do not need a thing.' But you do not realize that you are wretched, pitiful, poor, blind and naked" (Revelation 3:17). When a man boastfully describes himself as "financially independent," he is revealing a mind-set of an independent spirit in his relationship with God. Ever since Adam and Eve, humankind has instinctively been on a quest for self-sufficiency, rather than dependency. Think of hearing a two-year-old saying, "Me do," which in adult language means, "Mother, I'd rather do it myself." It is the innate sense of self-sufficiency inherent in all of us.

It is hard for us to admit our dependence upon God. We meet people every day who think they don't need God. Some are even so bold as to say that out loud. Every new shooting tragedy in our country should remind us that neither government, nor better education, nor more laws can fix the sin problem in the human heart. Satan feeds our ego by continuing to say: "You are not stupid. You can do it. You can get along without God. Furthermore, you can become 'like God, knowing good and evil' without God's help." However, Jesus taught, "Unless you change and become like little children, you will never enter the kingdom of heaven. Therefore, whoever humbles himself like this child is the greatest in the kingdom of heaven" (Matthew 18:3-4). Who is more dependent than a child?

In these last two paragraphs, I have highlighted what appears to be an age-old tension. A two-year-old child wants to be independent yet is so dependent. We never outgrow this tension because the sense of independence is an illusion. For most adults this fantasy has become a reality after so many years of thinking it is true, but it is still a false impression.

LET'S LOOK AT JESUS

Think of Jesus as a helpless babe in a manger. Think about the second person of the Trinity needing someone to carry Him those first months of His earthly existence. He depended upon someone to feed Him as a baby because He could not feed Himself.

Think of Him on the cross when He said, "Into your hands I commit my spirit." He was totally dependent upon the Father to raise Him from the dead. Concerning His ministry, Jesus made it clear: "I tell you the truth, the Son can do nothing by himself; he can do only what he sees his Father doing, because whatever the Father does the Son also does" (John 5:19). Moreover, in John 6:57 He said, "I live because of the Father, so the one who feeds on me will live because of me." (The phrase "feeds on" is another way of describing what it means to receive Christ into our lives by faith.) Jesus, in His humanity, needed others, just as we do. In Matthew 26:38, Jesus said, "My soul is overwhelmed with sorrow to the point of death. Stay here and keep watch with me."

Jesus became poor. "For you know the grace of our Lord Jesus Christ, that though he was rich, yet for your sakes he became poor, so that you through his poverty might become rich" (2 Corinthians 8:9). Was that poverty related to the fact that He had no place to lay His head? Was it about the need to borrow a donkey for His triumphal ride into Jerusalem? Was it about the fact that they needed to borrow a tomb in which to place His crucified body? (Incidentally, that was a smart financial move, since He wouldn't need it very long!) Or, was it about His attitude of dependency?

It is clear that Jesus lived His life here on earth in dependence upon the Father and the Holy Spirit. Andrew Murray wrote, "When He [Jesus] emptied Himself of His Divine glory, He laid aside the free use of His Divine attributes. He needed thus as a man to live by faith; He needed to wait on the Father for such communications of wisdom and power, as it pleased the Father to impart to Him. He was entirely dependent on the Father; His life was hid in God." An attitude of dependence is a Christ-like quality.

LET'S SEE DEPENDENCE IN RELATION TO OUR SALVATION

Every human being needs to be saved, and there is nothing we can do to save ourselves. Christ did for us what we cannot do for ourselves. I have yet to meet a person who claims to have lived a perfect life and has never done anything wrong. The issue is—what to do about it. Our natural mind-set is: "I'd rather fix it myself." But I can't. I can't remove one sin from my record that God keeps in heaven. I am not self-sufficient; only God is. He alone draws life from nothing but Himself. A wonder of God's grace is that we are made "partakers of the divine nature" (2 Peter 1:4 KJV). There are "communicable attributes" in God's nature which are imparted to us in a finite degree by the Holy Spirit when we are born again. Examples are: wisdom, goodness, holiness, justice, mercy, grace. There are also "incommunicable attributes" in God's nature such as self-existence, self-sufficiency, infinity, immutability, sovereignty, omnipotence, omniscience, and omnipresence. The problem is that we think we can make ourselves like God with attributes that are His alone. This is one of the worst manifestations of our delusional attitude of independence and self-sufficiency.

The Jews to whom Jesus spoke that day were proud of many things including their religious achievements, their ceremonial activities, their sacrifices they offered to God, their zeal for the law, their position as God's chosen people, and their self-righteousness. We all have, by nature, the same attitude, thinking we should get high marks for our goodness. However, God calls that goodness "filthy rags." If God deems our righteousness as "filthy rags," how does He regard our unrighteousness? As hard as it may be, the first step in coming to God for salvation is acknowledging our spiritual poverty.

When Jesus told a parable about the Pharisee who "stood up and prayed about himself" and the tax collector who "beat his breast and said 'God, have mercy on me, a sinner'" (Luke 18:9-14), He told it for those "who were confident of their own righteousness." "Poor in spirit" means we come to God with the attitude of a beggar. A curious thing is happening in our society today. People, even respectable corporations, are not ashamed to take welfare handouts, entitlements, and bailouts. Yet, down deep, there is a sinful pride that keeps people from begging God for help. There are proud panhandlers (people who make a career of being parasites and arrogantly expect handouts) but no proud beggars (destitute, poverty-stricken people who are grateful for any help). This attitude of dependence is the opposite of Pharisaic self-righteousness. Jesus said, "Unless your righteousness surpasses that of the Pharisees and the teachers of the law, you will certainly not enter the kingdom of heaven" (Matthew 5:20).

Philosophers tell us, "Know thyself." But the Bible tells us, "The heart is deceitful above all things and beyond cure. Who can understand it?" (Jeremiah 17:9) We need an objective mirror to see ourselves as we really are. The Bible is that mirror. It says, there is "no one righteous, not even one" . . . "no one who seeks God" . . . "no one who does good, not even one" . . . "there is no fear of God" (Romans 3:10-18). The Bible says we are "without strength," "dead in trespasses and sins," "blind," "lost," and "helpless." To think accurately about ourselves, we must see ourselves as God sees us. Confession is saying the same thing about ourselves that God says. If we do not accept what God says in His Word about sin, then we will find ourselves competing with others over who gets to decide right and wrong. Until we see ourselves as clothed with "filthy rags" (Isaiah 64:6), we cannot be clothed with the righteousness of Christ.

This condition is what theologians call "total depravity." That does not mean that everyone is as sinful as he or she can be. Some neighbors are better than others. For example, I'd much rather have a neighbor who has high moral principles than someone who is a pedophile. There are lots of good people around, but when it comes to being good enough to get into heaven, "There is no one who does good, not even one." Total depravity means that the image of God in man has been polluted, perverted, and distorted, and each person is rendered incapable of saving himself or herself. In the heart of every person there is the seed of every conceivable sin. Just because you have not committed the worst of sins, it does not mean that God can accept you into His heaven. James writes, "For whoever keeps the whole law and yet stumbles at just one point is guilty of breaking all of it" (James 2:10).

> Total depravity means that the image of God in man has been polluted, perverted, and distorted, and each person is rendered incapable of saving himself or herself.

The eighteenth-century Age of Enlightenment had a dramatic effect on human reasoning culminating in the following rationale: human beings are basically good; God is good; and since people are like God, then God is like people. In the process, the difference between the Creator and the created is blurred. As a result, we lose our sense of depravity and our dependence upon God for our salvation. However, when we see God as He is, we need to respond like Isaiah, "Woe to me. . . . I am ruined" (Isaiah 6:5) and like Paul, "I know that nothing good lives in me, that is, in my sinful nature" (Romans 7:18). When you meet a person who is beginning to understand this, then you know that God is graciously working in that life by His Holy Spirit.

The word "saved" is a thrilling word that stirs up all kinds of celebration and joy. When a child is trapped in a burning building, the fireman risks his life, rushes into the building, and returns with the child in his arms. The watching crowd cheers loudly when someone shouts, "The child is saved!"

Jesus "came to seek and save what was lost" (Luke 19:10). Unfortunately, people resent that idea because it implies they are in danger and need a Savior. I'm amazed that "Amazing Grace" is still such a popular gospel song when it includes the line, "That saved a wretch like me." We are lost before we know it, and nobody is more lost than the person who is lost and doesn't know it. Nobody is sicker than the man filled with cancer but refuses to go to a doctor for a thorough physical exam and goes on thinking he is well. I believe the number one reason why people are not saved is that they are too proud to admit they need a Savior and refuse to come to Christ in prayer as beggars. We hear people give witness to receiving Christ as their personal Savior, but before that happened, they had to come to a crisis point in their lives where they saw themselves as "poor in spirit." In total dependence upon Christ, they cried out for mercy. This is like the prodigal son in the pigpen who "came to his senses," went back home, admitted to his father his total depravity, and humbly acknowledged that he was no longer worthy to be called a son. This kind of thinking is indicative of someone who is humbly dependent.

God has a wonderful plan for our salvation. It is a plan that not only results in our salvation but, more important, ensures that God can be "just and the one who justifies those who have faith in Jesus" (Romans 3:26). This perfect plan all revolves around the death of Christ on the cross. Unless God provides salvation through the substitutionary, atoning death of His Son, we cannot be saved. That's how dependent we are upon Him.

The fundamental question of religion is: how does a just and holy God take a sinner into heaven without violating His justice? It is clear from Scripture that we can do nothing to atone for our own sins. Psalm 49:7-8 states, "No man can redeem the life of another or give to God a ransom for him—the ransom for a life is costly, no payment is ever enough." Only the vicarious death of Jesus Christ answers the question about how to get into God's heaven. A basic law of heaven is: "The soul who sins is the one who will die" (Ezekiel 18:4, 20), and "without the shedding of blood there is no forgiveness" (Hebrews 9:22). For God to remain just and holy, He cannot simply overlook our indiscretions and let sins go unpunished. Some try to rationalize that "He [God] knows how we are formed, he remembers that we are dust" (Psalm 103:14) and therefore will tolerate our sins. The reason we can be forgiven is not that God understands us, but that Christ died for us as our substitute. God's love motivated Him to provide a substitute that would satisfy His righteous demands and make it possible for the believing sinner to go unpunished for his or her own sins.

This concept of "substitutionary atonement" was introduced by God in the Old Testament. It started all the way back in the Garden of Eden. An animal was killed. Blood was shed. "The LORD God made garments of skin for Adam and his wife and clothed them" (Genesis 3:21). Another picture is found in Genesis 22 when God provided a ram for Abraham to sacrifice instead of his son Isaac. Exodus and Leviticus are filled with instructions about killing a lamb without spot or blemish as a "trespass offering" to make atonement for sin. Every year, on the Day of Atonement (Yom Kippur), the high priest would enter the "inner room" but "never without blood" (Hebrews 9:7). However, the blood of animals could not take away the sins of people (see Hebrews 10:4).

Then, John the Baptist introduced Jesus as "The Lamb of God, who takes away the sin of the world!" (John 1:29) "He entered the Most Holy Place once for all by his own blood, having obtained eternal redemption" (Hebrews 9:12). His death on the cross satisfied the righteous demands of the holy God. So now God can declare the believing sinner to be righteous. Our only hope is in the ransom Christ paid for sinners. He is the only one who can pay the price of the debt owed to God. We need the blood of Christ to appease God's wrath. That is not intended to paint a picture of God being a fuming tyrant in heaven unwilling to calm down until He gets His pound of flesh. Jesus did not play the part of a dysfunctional peacemaker between disobedient children and an angry father. Remember—God so loved us that He gave His Son. He sent Him to die for us. He is for us, not against us. He wants us happy—His way.

In Psalms 32 and 51, David pleaded guilty and begged for God's mercy. David clearly saw his sins as transgressions against God, and God alone. An old Puritan, in *The Valley of Vision*, wrote, "Let me never forget that the heinousness of sin lies not so much in the nature of the sin committed, as in the greatness of the Person sinned against." Jesus did not die for man's sin against man, but for man's sin against God. (That does not mean we no longer need to make things right with someone we have wronged. We'll come back to that in a later chapter.) It is imperative to understand that salvation comes when we humble ourselves before the Lord and admit to Him that we have sinned against Him and Him alone.

Beyond all that was accomplished at Calvary, it is the Father who draws us to the Son (John 6:44). It is the Holy Spirit who convicts us of sin (John 16:8), opens the eyes of the spiritually blinded, awakens us to our need for Christ, and reveals Him to us. Unless that happens, we will remain lost in our sins. That's how dependent we are upon God for our salvation.

There are people who go to church and want to leave feeling good about themselves, and they can! What will make a person feel good more than agreeing with God about sin and asking for forgiveness and experiencing God's cleansing? However, in a superficial way, people don't like hearing a message about sin or human depravity and the fact that they are "poor in spirit." Sadly, some leave the service down on themselves, feeling there is no hope because they want to be self-sufficient and "do it myself." Sometimes preachers feel this pressure and want people to feel good. So, the gospel is diluted and made palatable to the natural man. The unspoken message is: If you just admit that you made some mistakes and aren't as good as you should be—you don't need to see yourself as a beggar in abject spiritual poverty.

But let's start where Jesus began with the Beatitudes. To be reminded of my sin and depravity is not an unhealthy exercise, unless it is divorced from the grace of God. When we underestimate the horridness of sin, we also undervalue the grace of God. There is not a sin I am incapable of committing. The power of positive thinking, self-realization, and self-actualization are not going to cut it. I am at the end of my rope. I am out of options. I cry with Paul, "What a wretched man I am! Who will rescue me from this body of death?" (Romans 7:24) The answer—Christ and Christ alone!

LET'S SEE DEPENDENCE IN RELATION TO OUR SPIRITUAL FORMATION

Humility is the starting point and represents the first step in the Christian life, but it also is required for every subsequent step. We cannot move on to the rest of the Beatitudes without this foundational attitude of humble dependence upon God for the power to live as we ought. This perspective is captured in Paul's admonition to the "foolish Galatians": "Are you so foolish? After beginning with the Spirit, are you now trying to attain your goal by human effort?" (Galatians 3:3) Jesus said, "It is not the healthy who need a doctor, but the sick" (Mark 2:17). We can begin our Christian journey by admitting our desperate need for salvation and come to the Great Physician as a beggar. Later, we can slip back into our old mind-set and think we don't need to depend on Him anymore. (This is what we do with those in the medical profession—grateful that we have doctors when we need them, but even more grateful when we think we don't need them.) We are never in greater danger than when all appears to be going well and we think we have no more need of God.

There are people who have a strong will and dogged determination and accomplish amazing things by what appears to be their own strength. There are self-help books, 12-step regimens, and a host of other programs that operate on the premise—if you can dream it, you can achieve it. Some people do accomplish great things. However, nobody can "form Christ" in themselves. That is the work of the Holy Spirit. We desperately need the grace of God, which is His strength made perfect in our weakness. Obviously, spiritual formation requires our participation, but we must continually be aware of our weakness and depend on His strength. Paul said, "By the grace of God I am what I am" (1 Corinthians 15:10). There is nothing more deadly than self-reformation. "God gives grace to the humble"—to those with the mind-set of continuous dependence upon Him. That's how we grow spiritually and become fully devoted disciples of Christ. My deepest prayer is that this book will be used by God to help many people on their spiritual journey of "Christ being formed in you."

LET'S SEE DEPENDENCE IN RELATION TO OUR SPIRITUAL MINISTRY

When it comes to fruitful ministry, Christ made it perfectly clear: "Apart from me you can do nothing" (John 15:5). Paul said, "I worked harder than all of them—yet not I, but the grace of God that was with me" (1 Corinthians 15:10). He wrote in 2 Corinthians 4:7, "But we have this treasure [this ministry he describes in verses 1-6] in jars of clay to show that this all-surpassing power is from God and not from us." Thank God! He uses weak, broken vessels so that His glorious power may be seen. His work in us to "conform us to the image of His Son" is designed to make the messenger like the message. In other words, we walk the talk. We must continually remember that the power is not in the argument of the messenger, but in the power of the message. Paul said, "I came to you in weakness and fear, and with much trembling. My message and my preaching were not with wise and persuasive words, but with a demonstration of the Spirit's power, so that your faith might not rest on men's wisdom, but on God's power" (1 Corinthians 2:3-5). We abandon ourselves to the all-sufficient resources of God's grace.

The story of Jesus' raising Lazarus from the dead serves as an insightful illustration for us. Lazarus's condition was like the unconverted who are dead in their sins. We can no more raise a spiritually dead person to life than the people standing there that day could bring Lazarus back to life. Only Jesus could call Lazarus out of the tomb. However, He did say, "Take off the grave clothes and let him go" (John 11:44). We, too, have responsibilities in ministry similar to helping others get rid of the "grave clothes" of the old life.

Our dependence upon God for effective ministry cannot be an excuse for passivity. It's like the farmer who needs to plow up the fallow ground, plant the seed, water and fertilize it, but who can't make it grow. In fact, he doesn't even know how it grows (Mark 4:26-29). Paul said, "I planted the seed, Apollos watered it, but God made it grow" (1 Corinthians 3:6). And it is also true that it is God who gives us the spiritual strength to do our part.

Maybe we need to think again about how the New Testament describes ministry. The church is commissioned with the task of preaching the gospel to every creature, discipling people in all nations, baptizing them in the name of the Father and of the Son and of the Holy Spirit, and teaching them to do all Jesus commanded (see Matthew 28:18-20 and Mark 16:15). The gospel must be demonstrated and declared. Both must be done in total dependence upon the power of the Holy Spirit, not upon our own strength and ability.

I remember a preacher years ago saying, "God receives what we give to Him without reservation. What He receives, He cleanses. What He cleanses, He fills with the Holy Spirit. What He fills with the Holy Spirit, He uses for His glory." That sequence never changes. If we want "gold, silver, and precious stones" rather than "wood, hay, and stubble," it must be God working through us, not our trying to serve God in our own strength. On the outside, the activities may look the same, but the critical difference is on the inside where we must know that we are totally dependent upon God for fruitful ministry.

There are many practical, temporal things that can be done "in His name" which will open the door for sharing the gospel. An understanding of God's working through us means that even giving a cup of cold water in His strength will not go unrewarded (Matthew 10:42). Down through church history believers have found that alleviating the physical suffering of people has given them an entrée to preaching the gospel. However, over time, these activities can become an end in themselves rather than a means to the end. It is easy to gradually—almost undiscernibly—slip into a mode of operation that is independent of God.

Even more serious, people can look from the outside and conclude that church evangelistic ministry is focused on humanitarian causes, social issues, the betterment of human institutions, etc. Read typical church bulletins today and you might get the impression that the outreach ministry of the church is all about doing such things as providing backpacks for underprivileged school children, going on short-term mission trips to help build church buildings, doing housework for disabled or elderly people, etc. These are good things and they need to be done, but they may be only temporal and not lead to the eternal. The goal of Christian ministry is not to improve the temporal well-being of people but "to open their eyes and turn them from darkness to light, and from the power of Satan to God, so that they may receive forgiveness of sins and a place among those who are sanctified by faith in me" (Acts 26:18). If we as Christ's followers don't do this, who will? "For what will it profit a man if he gains the whole world, and loses his own soul?" (Mark 8:36 NKJV) What does it profit if we educate people and fill their stomachs, but they end in hell?

Ed Erny, with One Mission Society, wrote in an article entitled "Keeping the Shell and Discarding the Kernel": "Today there seems to be a disconcerting tendency for missionary candidates to seek to serve Christ in almost any capacity but direct evangelism." Dr. Donald McGavran, the "father" of the modern church growth movement, wrote the following to mission executives: "Careful research into what is actually done by missionaries on mission fields has revealed beyond the shadow of a doubt that most monies sent out from America by mission executives go to carry on good works with little evangelistic effect." The scholarly and devout missionary statesman Bishop Stephen Neill, after a lifetime devoted to missions, came to the conclusion that "personal conversion is at the heart of missions." Viewing with misgiving the growing emphasis in churches on social issues, he declared, "Those who start at the social end never seem to get to the gospel, whereas those who start with the gospel sometimes accomplish, without knowing or intending it, the social revolution."

> I submit that the root problem is a very subtle form of pride that makes people want to do something on their own.

A newspaper reporter once wrote, "I can see nothing whatever in D. L. Moody to account for his marvelous work." When Moody read the report, he chuckled, "Why, that is the very secret of the movement. There is nothing in it that can explain it but the power of God. The work is God's, not mine." God chooses "the lowly things of this world and the despised things . . . so that no one may boast before him" (1 Corinthians 1:28-29).

I submit that the root problem is a very subtle form of pride that makes people want to do something on their own, apart from total dependence upon God. All these humanitarian/social/institutional things—as well as "direct evangelism"—must be done by the strength which God supplies. The fact is, the humanitarian/social/institutional things can be done by people who make no profession of being born again and without the enabling work of the Holy Spirit. A strong case could be made for this kind of ministry being "dead works" that are not of faith and cannot produce life (see Hebrews 6:1; 9:14). Henry Blackaby would say these are "works not initiated and empowered by God." They can be rabbit trails that sidetrack us from the work that God wants to do in us and through us. Jesus made it clear: "The Spirit gives life; the flesh counts for nothing" (John 6:63).

Do we run the risk of reducing Christian ministry to the level of human attainment? It is easy to become content with our busyness, even if no one "has crossed over from death to life" (John 5:24). The world needs to see the power of God that changes lives, not just the work of our hands. Hudson Taylor, the founder of the China Inland Mission (now OMF International), said, "Realize that the work of God does not mean so much man's work for God, as God's own work through man." Jesus said, "I will build my church." He also said, "Go into all the world and preach the good news to all creation" (Mark 16:15). However, Christ admonished the apostles not to undertake this mission until they were "clothed with power from on high" (Luke 24:49; Acts 1:8). It is "'Not by might nor by power, but by my Spirit,' says the LORD Almighty" (Zechariah 4:6).

God refuses to use our most spectacular gifts and unique qualifications until we are weaned from reliance on them. Every day we must recognize how utterly dependent we are upon God's enabling for fruitful ministry that glorifies Him. Otherwise, we will be like the Israelites whom God warned—"You may say to yourself, 'My power and the strength of my hands have produced this wealth for me.' But remember the LORD your God, for it is he who gives you the ability to produce wealth" (Deuteronomy 8:17-18). What a freeing thing it is to rest in God's power that flows through us as "channels of blessing" and not feel the pressure of producing results!

We walk an invisible line between excellent training for ministry and a refusal to depend on our own ability. We plan, strategize, budget, dream, but we go astray if we try to find success in our own strength. Others looking on from the outside may not see the difference, but we must know in our heart of hearts that we are totally dependent upon God.

IN SUMMARY: "If anyone serves, he should do it with the strength God provides, so that in all things God may be praised through Jesus Christ. To him be the glory and the power forever and ever. Amen" (1 Peter 4:11). In this context, I understand responsibility to mean that my role is response and God gives the ability.

Oh, that we might see again a "Great Awakening" kind of revival in our churches. Oh, that we might experience a new fervency and earnestness as we cry out to God for revival! Oh, that there would be a strong sense of the manifest presence of God when His people meet for worship! Oh, that God would give us a holy boldness in our witnessing! Oh, that God would enable us to be more like Christ so that people would ask us the reason for our hope (1 Peter 3:15). Oh, that we would see God change lives, heal sick bodies, restore marriages, and solve problems that have gone unsolved for years! Oh, that people in our communities might be moved by what they see God doing in our churches! Oh, that people would see our good works and glorify God, not us! All of these experiences would demonstrate that we are not doing ministry in the energy of the flesh but in the power of the Holy Spirit.

LET'S SEE DEPENDENCE IN RELATION TO PRAYER

Prayer is to be the first work of every believer. It is to be our first response, not our last resort. There is a broad description of prayer that includes conversation with God, friend to friend; thanksgiving to God; daily devotions in which we express our worship to God; etc. The narrower definition of prayer is "asking and receiving." Prayer is God's way for us to obtain what we need from Him (James 4:2). This is not "saying a prayer" like children sending a wish list to Santa Claus. It is not sending up a trial balloon and hoping it works its magic so that everything works out as we would like. True praying is not to be taken lightly, but in utter dependence upon God we cry out to Him for help in time of need.

This kind of prayer occurs when we depend upon God. Prayerlessness occurs when we depend upon ourselves. A praying church has learned to depend upon God. Success in ministry is dependent upon dependent prayer. A pastor recently did a small, unscientific survey asking other pastors to describe the church they served and other churches they knew about. The summary of the results was stated in three words—prayerlessness, apathy, and self-centeredness. Too many churches are content with superficial experiences and never get to the place of crying out to God in earnest, fervent prayer. (Study verses such as Psalms 3:4; 9:12; 56:9-10; 86:3). "Pray without ceasing" means, among other things, having a perpetual mind-set of total dependence upon God. God still says, "If my people will humble themselves and pray" (2 Chronicles 7:14). Prayer is a telltale sign of living this Beatitude individually and as a church.

LET'S SEE DEPENDENCE IN RELATION TO GRATITUDE

Since we "have nothing but what we have received," it is only appropriate that we be continually thankful. Since "every good and perfect gift is from above" (James 1:17), our gratitude needs to be directed to God as that source from above. Ingratitude is a grievous sin. Not to be thankful is to take the first step down the slippery slope that leads to God's giving us "over to a depraved mind" (Romans 1:18-32). It is pride that keeps us from saying "thank you" to God and others. Gratitude is the opposite of discontent, dissatisfaction, grumbling, complaining, taking things for granted, etc. True beggars are grateful for every gift. That certainly needs to be true of us when we think of the wonderful gift of eternal life, His grace that is sufficient, the great privilege of being "laborers together with Him," and answers to prayer. We are to "offer the sacrifice of praise to God continually, that is, the fruit of your lips giving thanks to his name" (Hebrews 13:15 KJV). This humble attitude is a great way to develop thought patterns of humility and to prevent us from becoming proud.

LET'S SEE DEPENDENCE IN RELATION TO THE CHURCH

God has designed His church so that every part of the body of Christ needs every other part. "Under his direction, the whole body is fitted together perfectly. As each part does its own special work, it helps the other parts grow, so that the whole body is healthy and growing and full of love" (Ephesians 4:16 NLT). Paul wrote to the Corinthians, "The eye cannot say to the hand, 'I don't need you!' And the head cannot say to the feet, 'I don't need you.' . . . If one part suffers, every part suffers with it; if one part is honored, every part rejoices with it" (1 Corinthians 12:21, 26). The Bible teaches us as members in the body of Christ to be interdependent, not independent. This mind-set of dependency is essential for the church to function as it should. It means doing all the "one another" ministries taught in the New Testament. It means having the accountability that church membership should provide. That means confronting one another in love and responding with a humble, teachable spirit, because others can see our flaws more easily than we can. It means sharing in the common life of the church. Stewardship is a much bigger subject than tithing. However, understanding that we "have nothing but what we have received" and that God owns it all is the first step in being a good steward who brings a "collection" to the church on "the first day of every week" (1 Corinthians 16:1-2). This is just another way we show our dependence upon God and live out the first Beatitude.

Holy Father, help me to see that it is impossible to become more and more like Christ unless I acknowledge my spiritual poverty. Work in my life until I am absolutely dependent upon You as Jesus was when He was here on earth. Enable me also to see that, in Your Son, You have provided everything I need for "life and godliness" (2 Peter 1:3). Deliver me from a proud spirit that thinks I can get along without You and everybody else. Daily show me all the areas of life in which this attitude of Christ-like dependence gives me opportunities to be a witness for You. Amen.

In the next chapter we will look at the second part of humility!

PERSONAL-REFLECTION QUESTIONS

- Do you understand why you are totally dependent upon the death and resurrection of Christ for your salvation well enough that you can effectively communicate that fact to other people? If not, what should you do?
- How do you know that you are doing ministry in the strength which God supplies?
- How is your prayer life an expression of dependence upon God?
- How do you express your dependence upon the other members of your church?

GROUP-DISCUSSION QUESTIONS

- How should we as Christians feel about the "welfare mentality" in our nation?
- How should we distinguish between healthy and unhealthy kinds of dependence?
- What do you think about "the number one reason why people are not saved"?
- What do you think about the growing emphasis on humanitarian activity as outreach?
- What are some ways we can help people today to see their spiritual poverty when it comes to getting into heaven?

3

The Blessedness of Being Poor in Spirit! – Part 2

Blessed are the poor in spirit, for theirs is the kingdom of heaven.
(Matthew 5:3)

We have just considered one part of being "poor in spirit" or humble, which is the mind-set of *dependence*. Now we consider another aspect of humility which is the mind-set of *submission*.

Genuine humility is not putting yourself down. It is putting yourself under proper authority.

Paul said, "I am the least of the apostles" (1 Corinthians 15:9); "I am less than the least of all God's people" (Ephesians 3:8); I am the chief of sinners (1 Timothy 1:15 NKJV). If we have our chronology right concerning when these Epistles were written, the longer Paul lived, the less he thought of himself. That was not because he became more depraved, but because as he drew closer to Christ, the contrast became more obvious. Paul was not putting himself down. Instead, he was gaining a more accurate picture of himself in relationship with Christ.

Humility is a basic Christ-like attitude—and it is extremely tricky. Since the "heart is deceitful above all things," you and I can easily deceive ourselves into thinking we are humble, when we are not. How do you know for sure that you are totally dependent upon God to enable you for effective ministry? Are you sure that you are not relying on your own strength? How do you know for sure that you are genuinely humble and not putting on a facade to impress people? You may deflect praise to God and to others who help you, but over time you come to realize that people think more highly of you when you do that. Suddenly, your projected humility can become a point of pride.

Here's what Charles Spurgeon had to say, "Pride is self-deceit. Those who are sure that they have no pride are probably the proudest of all. Those who are proud of their humility are proud indeed. The confidence that we are not deceived may only prove the completeness of the deception under which we labor." Andrew Murray once said, "Humility is that grace that, when you know you have it, you have lost it." He also said, "Humility is not thinking meanly of yourself. It is simply not thinking of yourself at all!"

I have observed that if we think of "poor in spirit" only as being a dependent beggar, we will have only a partial understanding of this Beatitude. The Bible teaches, "Humble yourselves, therefore, under God's mighty hand, that he may lift you up in due time" (1 Peter 5:6). In that verse, "humble" is in the verb form and requires action. That biblical instruction typically leads to doing something such as putting ourselves down so we appear to be humble. But if we humble ourselves by putting ourselves under proper authority, we will get a more complete picture of what it means to be genuinely humble. In fact, I believe this should be the litmus test for humility. How do I typically respond when someone with proper authority tells me what to do?

> I believe this should be the litmus test for humility: How do I typically respond when someone with proper authority tells me what to do?

This concept of submission is grossly misunderstood in our modern North American culture. It is contrary to our human nature. From the day we were born, we have wanted our own way. It is a basic part of our sinful nature. Who taught a child to have a temper tantrum? It is not just the "strong-willed child" who wants to control everything. We all want to be in charge somewhere. The essence of pride is contained in such statements as, "I will" or "I am the master of my fate." No wonder the idea of submitting to authority is foreign to us. We don't like it. Yet it is the most fundamental attitude in the life of Christ and in the life of a Christ-follower. If we are going to get this Beatitude right, we must deal with the issue of authority.

How do we get from "poor in spirit" to humility and on to submission? Good question. The first step is rather straightforward. Go back over the definitions of "poor in spirit" in the previous chapter. I've never met a proud beggar. Every book I've read and every sermon I've heard about the Beatitudes uses the word "humility" to describe this basic attitude. Going from humility to submission requires a little more digging. Obviously, beggars are not in charge of very much. "Beggars can't be choosers." The word for "poor" also means to "bow before" or "cower." God says, "I will bless those who have humble and contrite hearts, who *tremble at my word*" [Italics added] (Isaiah 66:2 NLT). Bible passages such as James 4:6-9 and 1 Peter 5:5-6 certainly tie humility and submission together. If pride is the opposite of humility, and pride includes rebellion and self-rule, then humility would include submission.

WHAT DOES SUBMISSION MEAN?

Submission means to be subject to someone else and to put oneself under proper authority. It is a military term where, within various ranks of authority, I obey those who are over me. It also includes the idea of joyfully and voluntarily adapting to the plans and wishes of another person. Therefore, it is allowing someone (God or someone to whom He has delegated authority over me) to make a decision that affects my life and responding with joyful obedience. Most people struggle with the idea of "joyful." They want to go through the external motions of obeying without the inner attitude of submission. But doing it joyfully makes submission something much deeper and insures that it is an attitude, not just an action.

WHAT DOES SUBMISSION NOT MEAN?

- It is *not* acquiescence or passive resignation which is a basic weakness of character rather than being strong in the strength which God supplies. It is not like the little boy whose mother told him to sit down. When he finally did, he said, "I'm sitting down on the outside, but I'm still standing up on the inside."
- It is *not* blind obedience. This Beatitude is a thought pattern that requires the use of our minds. Although much of what the Bible says is counterintuitive, that doesn't mean it is impossible to understand and believe. We don't leave our brains at the door while living the Christian life.
- It is *not* selective submission. When it comes to proper authority, I don't get to choose which regulations or assignments I will obey. Think about it. If I could make that choice, then I would be in charge.
- It is *not* about bullies or even people in authority forcing me to obey. Submission is a voluntary attitude.
- It is *not* a "blank check" for obeying all human beings all the time. It is putting myself under proper authority. It recognizes that delegated authority is strictly "limited authority." A person deputized in one county cannot exercise authority in another county. A wife is not to obey her husband when he tells her to do something that God's Word forbids. Peter and John said to the Sanhedrin, "Judge for yourselves whether it is right in God's sight to obey you rather than God. For we cannot help speaking about what we have seen and heard" (Acts 4:19-20). With an

attitude of submission they had to obey God and not man, even if it meant going to jail. (We'll get back to this when we get to the subject of persecution.)

- It is *not* without the responsibility of respectfully appealing to authority. The early leaders of our country were on solid biblical ground when they set up the Court of Appeals system. Go all the way back to Paul who obviously suffered persecution and all kinds of hardship. But read about his trial before Felix and Festus (Acts 24 and 25). He said, "I appeal to Caesar!" And in Acts 27 we read about Paul's sailing to Rome to appear before Caesar. Likewise, we need an attitude of submission that includes the responsibility to make as strong an appeal as possible. Then, unless the decision by those in authority involves action that is forbidden by God, we say, "Whatever you finally decide, I will joyfully obey." That puts tremendous responsibility on the one in authority—which is as it should be.

SEE SUBMISSION IN THE LIFE OF JESUS

Jesus was sent by the Father. He came not to do His own will, but the will of the Father who sent Him (John 6:38). He did not speak His own words but the words His Father gave Him to speak (John 14:10). "He learned obedience from what he suffered" (Hebrews 5:8). He said, "My food . . . is to do the will of him who sent me" (John 4:34). Paul wrote, "Now I want you to realize that the head of every man is Christ, and the head of the woman is man, and the head of Christ is God" (1 Corinthians 11:3). The most vivid scene showing this attitude in the life of Jesus happened in the garden of Gethsemane. There He prayed, "Father, if you are willing, take this cup from me; yet not my will, but yours be done" (Luke 22:42). In Pilate's hall, "When they hurled their insults at him, he did not retaliate; when he suffered, he made no threats. Instead, he entrusted himself to him who judges justly" (1 Peter 2:23). "He humbled himself and became obedient to death—even death on a cross" (Philippians 2:8). Everything about Jesus' life was subservient to the will of His Father. This was (and is) His "mind." This attitude of submission is a Christ-like quality. If we want to be like Jesus, we must have this same attitude of submission.

Let's consider two areas of submission—to God and to one another.

SUBMIT TO GOD

Since God is love and does only what is right and good, submission should be easy. However, humankind continues to stubbornly insist on being the master of its own fate. The idea of being in control of our own life is really a myth.

How much of what is really important about our life do we really control? With hardness of heart, Pharaoh defiantly said, "Who is the LORD, that I should obey him?" (Exodus 5:2) Although most people are afraid to say that out loud, they live with that mind-set.

Some try to get around the idea of submitting to God by foolishly saying there is no God (atheism). Others say they believe in a god who jump-started everything in the universe and then let it run on its own (deism). The fact is that if the God of the Bible exists (theism), then He continually holds everything together from the protons in microscopic cells to the billions of stars moving in the billions of galaxies without ever bumping into each other. Human beings and fallen angels are the only parts of God's creation that rebel against the Creator.

The book of Judges gives us a microcosm of human history in just a few quick generational cycles. The children of Israel entered the Promised Land knowing, loving, trusting, and obeying God. Over a relatively short period of time, they drifted away from God, abandoned Him for false gods, and "did as [they] saw fit" (Judges 21:25). God brought judgment on them in the form of oppression from other nations. When they finally repented of their sins and turned back to God, He forgave them and delivered them from the tyranny of their oppressors. They were back in harmony with God. Then that generation died, and the cycle began again. The choice is: be ruled by a tyrant or governed by a loving God. When will we learn? Read 2 Chronicles 12:1-16, especially verse 8.

> Human beings and fallen angels are the only parts of God's creation that rebel against the Creator.

GOD IS SOVEREIGN

If we can deal with this topic up front, then all the other issues related to submission fall into place. I don't profess to understand all questions regarding the sovereignty of God and the free will of man as that's above my pay grade. But I do know that we will never even begin to understand the subject of God's sovereignty if we don't begin with the first Beatitude. The fact is that God sovereignly oversees everything in the universe and "works out everything in conformity with the purpose of his will" (Ephesians 1:11). And what He wants for my life is far better than what I want. The sovereignty of God must be a deeply held conviction. We cannot worship a god who is not in control. There is no authority that is not under God's authority. Our sovereign God transcends creation (including human beings) and rules over it. He has established inviolable laws governing the universe and humankind. He holds us accountable to obey those laws and will be the final Judge to whom we answer.

THE BIBLE IS THE INSPIRED, AUTHORITATIVE WORD OF GOD

Everyone believes in absolutes—even those who insist there are no absolutes. (Saying "there are no absolutes" is an absolute statement.) The only difference is who gets to define the absolutes. Those with a mind-set of submission to God allow Him to declare what truth is through His inspired, authoritative, written Scripture. Some people come to the Bible out of curiosity to know what it says. They think they can learn about what God says and then decide whether or not to obey. However, Jesus said in John 7:17, "If anyone chooses to do God's will, he will find out whether my teaching comes from God or whether I speak on my own." In other words, we must have an attitude of commitment to doing God's will and then we will know God's will—not the other way around. Heresy does not come from people who humbly submit to God and seek to know and do His will; it comes from people who are in rebellion against God and try to use Scripture out of context to support their disobedience. Our attitude toward Scripture begins with the first Beatitude.

BEING FILLED WITH THE HOLY SPIRIT

Paul writes, "Do not be foolish, but understand what the Lord's will is. Do not get drunk on wine, which leads to debauchery. Instead be filled with the Spirit" (Ephesians 5:17-18). The person who is "drunk on wine" is controlled by that wine and does things he would not otherwise do. In similar fashion, we are to be filled with and controlled by the Holy Spirit and do good things that we could not otherwise do. Think about the ministry of the Holy Spirit in our lives. He guides us into all truth (John 16:13). "Those who are led by the Spirit of God are sons of God" (Romans 8:14). Paul expounds on this further in Romans 8:5-8: "Those who live according to the sinful nature have their minds set on what that nature desires; but those who live in accordance with the Spirit have their minds set on what the Spirit desires. The mind of sinful man is death, but the mind controlled by the Spirit is life and peace; the sinful mind is hostile to God. It does not submit to God's law, nor can it do so. Those controlled by the sinful nature cannot please God." Our attitude should be to submit to His control, not "quench the Spirit."

THE LORDSHIP OF CHRIST

I'm aware of at least some of the discussion as to whether a person can know Christ as Savior and not as Lord. Only God can see into a person's heart, but if I understand Scripture and this Beatitude, no one can have a pattern of deliberately, continually resisting the authority of Christ in their life and be in the kingdom of heaven. Our text ends with "for theirs is the kingdom of heaven" (Matthew 5:3). The force of the word "theirs" is *only* theirs. You cannot have a kingdom without a king. Christ is the King of His kingdom. As the King, He is Lord of all or not Lord at all.

Mary, the mother of our Lord, is a perfect illustration. When the angel told her that she would have a child and explained how it would happen, she said, "I am the Lord's servant . . . may it be to me as you have said" (Luke 1:38). In her song, Mary sang, "From now on all generations will call me blessed" (Luke 1:48). Our response 2000 years later is, Sure, Mary was happy—as she should be. She bore the Messiah. But remember all she endured as a young, pregnant, unmarried woman. Years later, she could say, with integrity, to the wedding planners in Cana, "Do whatever he tells you" (John 2:5). That is a demonstration of submission to the lordship of Christ.

BEING A SERVANT

The Bible uses many terms to describe followers of Christ: disciples, soldiers, saints, members of Christ's body, a chosen people, a royal priesthood, a holy nation, the bride of Christ, living stones, and branches. Interestingly, most often we are called servants. This figure of speech is another way to understand the attitude of submission. A servant is not in charge, the master is. Jesus exemplified this perspective when He said, "The Son of Man did not come to be served, but to serve" (Matthew 20:28). He gave us a key core value when He said, "The greatest among you will be your servant" (Matthew 23:11). In salvation we do not experience autonomy. We simply change masters.

As believers, we are "bond slaves" of Christ, humbly serving Him and those He has called us to serve for His sake. The concept of bond slave is much clearer in the original language of the New Testament than in English Bibles. It means to be devoted to someone to the disregard of one's own interests. It is not describing people who serve because they are forced by a slave owner to serve, but rather people who willingly, voluntarily give up their personal rights in order to serve someone else because of unconditional love and absolute loyalty. The bond servant goes beyond the call of duty. This mind-set is an essential thought pattern for the follower of Christ. Looking for ways to serve others without notice or reward is one of the telltale signs of humility.

BEING A LEADER

One of the greatest needs in our churches today is for more Christ-like leaders. Biblical leadership is not about being "King Tut" and swaying huge crowds with our oratory. It is more than exercising authority and wielding power. Jesus made it clear that the greatest among us is not the person who has the most power but the person who is serving the most people. We are to lead by serving and serve by leading. This kind of leadership is not about having people help you meet your goals but about you, as the leader, helping people meet their God-given vision and goals. Leaders do have authority and are responsible to make decisions, but they must do it with a humble, submissive, servant heart.

> Instead of thinking about power, we are to think about empowering others, so they can succeed in ministry and in living the Christ-like life.

A church leader's responsibility is "to equip God's people to do his work and build up the church, the body of Christ" (Ephesians 4:12 NLT). Paul instructed young Timothy, pastor of the church in Ephesus: "The things you have heard me say in the presence of many witnesses entrust to reliable men who will also be qualified to teach others" (2 Timothy 2:2). There was a time when I thought the hard part was to find "reliable men." Now I'm convinced that the hard part is to "entrust" to reliable men. That word means to let go of and put someone else in charge, as we do when we deposit money in the bank and trust the bank to make wise decisions with it. Instead of thinking about power, we are to think about empowering others, so they can succeed in ministry and in living the Christ-like life. In other words—we are to "make disciples."

PRAYER

Prayer is not only an expression of our dependence upon God (previous chapter) but is also an expression of our submission to the will of God. Prayer is not designed as a way to get what we want, but as a way to be involved in getting what God wants. This is how the Holy Spirit intercedes for us—"in accordance with God's will" (Romans 8:27). And "This is the confidence we have in approaching God: that if we ask anything according to his will, he hears us. And if we know that he hears us—whatever we ask—we know that we have what we asked of him" (1 John 5:14-15). James explains why some prayers are not answered—"When you ask, you do not receive, because you ask with wrong motives, that you may spend what you get on your pleasures" (James 4:3). We have learned that submission includes respectfully making an appeal; prayer is making that same kind of an appeal to God. That is what Jesus did when He prayed in the garden of Gethsemane. Simply stated, we cannot bypass this first Beatitude and hope to become a strong prayer warrior.

ACCEPT MYSELF AS GOD MADE ME

One of the foundational ways in which we submit to God is by acknowledging that He is the one who made us. We did not make ourselves (Psalm 100:3). Many people struggle with this truth because they just don't like themselves. "But who are you, O man, to talk back to God? Shall what is formed say to him who formed it, 'Why did you make me like this?' Does not the potter have the right to make out of the same lump of clay some pottery for noble purposes and some for common use?" (Romans 9:20-21) For instance, trying to be something we are not or giving too little or too much attention to personal appearance is not honoring to the God who made us.

The fact is, I am "fearfully and wonderfully made" by God (Psalm 139:14). God is the one "who made you, who formed you in the womb" (Isaiah 44:2). He is the one who determined who my parents would be; what time in history I would be born; what my race, nationality, gender, birth order, height, etc., would be. "From one man he made every nation of men, that they should inhabit the whole earth; and he determined the times set for them and the exact places where they should live" (Acts 17:26).

This understanding is also about accepting the spiritual gift(s) God has given to us "just as he determines" (1 Corinthians 12:11). When we reject what God made and what He has given to us, we are rejecting Him. This attitude is not about being proud of ourselves (we didn't make ourselves, so we have no bragging rights), but about being thankful to God for making us the way He did. I still remember the life-changing experience I had over forty-five years ago when a speaker challenged me not just to accept myself as God made me (which is different from accepting the mess I have made of what He made) but to actually thank God for making me the way He did. Jesus taught, "Love your neighbor as yourself" (Matthew 22:39). The more I understand and accept myself and thank God for the way He made me, the more I can love my neighbor as I love [accept] myself. Continually having this mind-set is essential for the attitude of submission.

PERSONAL DISCIPLINES

Beyond the basic areas we have already covered, we have the opportunity to voluntarily put ourselves under the control of personal standards. The internal mind-set of submission involved in properly obeying an officer of the law, for example, is the same attitude that triggers us to follow through in the routine, personal disciplines of everyday Christian living. There are times when God must humble us because we do not humble ourselves. I'd rather humble myself before God than be humbled and maybe even humiliated by Him. "If we judged ourselves, we would not come under judgment. When we are judged by the Lord, we are being disciplined so that we will not be condemned with the world" (1 Corinthians 11:31-32). This perspective is written in the context of how to celebrate the Lord's Supper, which is to be a regular time for self-examination. This aspect of submission teaches us that it is not optional, yet neither is it forced upon us.

Let me suggest some areas of personal discipline in our daily lives:

Holding personal biblical convictions. These are standards (not personal preferences) that are based on the Word of God which I set for myself and are consistently seen in my life. This could include such things as: How I will set aside one day in seven as unto the Lord to keep it holy; where will I draw the line when it comes to entertainment and amusement activities in which I will indulge; what kinds of food and how much I will eat.

Developing good habits. Have you noticed how easy it is to develop bad habits and how hard it is to break them—and how hard it is to develop good habits and how easy it is to break them? Good habits require personal discipline.

Reading, studying, and meditating in and memorizing Scripture. These are ways to "receive with meekness the engrafted word" (James 1:21 KJV). Grafting is done by splicing a branch from one tree into another tree. The branch will still have its own uniqueness but will receive its life and nourishment from the new tree. Something similar happens when we take in the Word of God.

Spending time in effective, fervent "closet praying" and group praying. Christlike praying in secret is the secret of Christ-like living in public.

Keeping vows I make to God and promises I make to people (Psalm 15:4b).

Thinking about such things as: "Whatever is true, whatever is noble, whatever is right, whatever is pure, whatever is lovely, whatever is admirable—if anything is excellent or praiseworthy—think about such things" (Philippians 4:8).

Having times of solitude so I can be still and know that God is God.

Maybe even include some practical activities such as:

Setting personal goals for spiritual development.

Adhering to a schedule. When people are habitually late, they have a mind-set of determining for themselves when to arrive rather than submitting to the appointed time.

Adhering to a budget. This means choosing to live within the means God has provided, honor Him with His tithe, provide for family needs, and demonstrate a balance between giving and saving with the remaining funds.

Having a sense of order in my life. "God is not a God of disorder" (1 Corinthians 14:33). Which do you think is more Christ-like—having a messy room or having a place for everything and everything in its place?

Following grammatical correctness in writing and speaking. Imagine the confusion we cause when we don't follow commonly accepted rules of grammar.

Some of you may be thinking—he's "quit preaching and gone to meddling." I'm only trying to show that every day we have many opportunities to live this Beatitude. There is great reward for exercising personal disciplines. Think of the runner who disciplines himself to run every day. It is agonizing at times, but he persists. Then the day comes when he experiences the sheer joy of running. Or think of the person who is learning a second language. It is hard work and requires discipline. However, hopefully, the day comes when she experiences the delight of thinking in that second language. Personal disciplines are not to bring us under bondage. They are to remain "personal" and not become something we force on other people. We are simply enabled by God to voluntarily put ourselves under our own authority. "The fruit of the Spirit is . . . self-control" (Galatians 5:22-23). We understand that freedom is not doing away with authority. It is having the strength and desire which God supplies to want to do what we ought to do—not out of duty, but willingly.

FEAR GOD

"Fear the Lord" is found over 160 times in the Bible! I was amazed to learn all the rewards and blessings that come with this emphasis in Scripture as well as all the consequences that come with not fearing the Lord. This is a wholesome, reverent respect for God rather than a destructive fear. Part of the meaning of the word "poor" is "to cower." The dictionary uses words such as grovel, cringe, recoil, and to shrink away from to define "cower." An example of its use in a sentence is: "They cowered at the sight of a gun." It is the kind of fear that a young teenager experiences when bullying goes on at school. Conversely, "fear the Lord" in the Bible means to bow your body down, not because you are scared, but because you are motivated by reverence and awe. The Bible gives many examples: Moses who bowed to the ground in the presence of God; Ezekiel who fell face down; and John who fell at Jesus' feet as though dead. It is being continually aware that "God . . . sees me" (Genesis 16:13), and every thought, word, and deed is open before Him to whom we are accountable. Think about how fearing God changes our lives. When we fear God, we will no longer need to fear anyone or anything else. Matthew 10:28 tells us: "Do not be afraid of those who kill the body but cannot kill the soul. Rather, be afraid of the One who can destroy both soul and body in hell." It is always to our advantage to be under God's authority.

"SUBMIT TO ONE ANOTHER OUT OF REVERENCE FOR CHRIST" (Ephesians 5:21)

Submitting to one another is one of the evidences of being filled with the Holy Spirit (Ephesians 5:18-21). This is not teaching some kind of "equal submission" that results in chaos because nobody knows who is in charge. "God is not a God of disorder"; He wants things done "in a fitting and orderly way" (1 Corinthians 14:33, 40). This is a mutual submission that is carefully explained in the remaining verses in Ephesians 5 and on into chapter 6, as well as in many other places in Scripture. I believe you can outline all the Bible teaches about submitting ourselves one to another under the following four headings:

- The Home—1 Corinthians 11:3; Ephesians 5:22–6:4; Colossians 3:18-21; Titus 2:5; 1 Peter 3:1-7
- The Government*—Romans 13:1-7; Titus 3:1-2; 1 Peter 2:13-17
- The Workplace—Ephesians 6:5-9; Colossians 3:22–4:1; Titus 2:9-10; 1 Peter 2:18-21
- The Church—Acts 20:28-31; 1 Timothy 5:17; Titus 1:5; Hebrews 13:7, 17; 1 Peter 5:1-6

*This could include all branches and levels of government and less formal community organizations such as: charities, service clubs, volunteer health organizations, amateur sports clubs, homeowners associations, boys and girls clubs and PTA.

When I study all these verses that relate to submitting to one another, I believe I can see the following principles that apply to all four areas of our lives. (There is no special order.)

- It is the responsibility of those in authority to care for and protect those whom they oversee.
- We are to be in submission, not just to avoid punishment, but to have a clear conscience.

- Those in positions of authority have been placed there by God.
- Those in positions of authority are God's servants.
- If we rebel against these authorities, we are rebelling against God and what He instituted.
- We are to submit to those in proper authority over us in the same way the church submits to Christ as its head.
- Submission does not just mean obedience. It also includes honoring and respecting those in authority.
- We are to submit to those in proper authority over us in the same way we submit to Christ.
- Everyone is created equal, but that does not change our responsibility to submit to those with God-ordained authority over us—just as Christ was equal with the Father but submitted to the Father as His head (1 Corinthians 11:3). We are not "second-class people" when we submit to those with proper authority over us.
- Submission means to please those in authority and not just when they are watching.
- Submission means to serve willingly as though we are serving the Lord and not just people.
- God has no favorites but, for our good, He does delegate authority over us.
- We are to submit, not as people-pleasers, but as God-pleasers.
- We are to submit to those in proper authority even when they are unkind and unreasonable because God is pleased when we do what we know is right and patiently endure unfair treatment.
- We are to submit to every authority for the Lord's sake.
- One responsibility of those in authority is to maintain order.
- Church leaders are responsible for training people in all that relates to submission in all four areas.
- Living in submission to those in authority produces an attractive life that others will want to emulate. In addition it will not bring reproach on the gospel, and the truth cannot be legitimately criticized.
- Living in submission is tied to humility and the grace which God gives to the humble enabling them to live this way.
- Those in positions of authority are ultimately accountable to God. Be warned about seeking positions of authority. Let God exalt you (Psalm 75:6-7).
- Those in authority are not to "lord it over people who are assigned to their care" but to lead by their good example.

Since the focus of this book is living the Beatitudes in the life of a local church and in everyday life, let's look at some practical applications of these principles.

Effective Church Structures

In a church setting, everyone needs to submit to someone else. Therefore, no one should be outside the umbrella of protective authority, doing his or her own thing. It is wise to have the governing documents of the church written in such a way that the "chain of command" is very clear. There is a wide spectrum of policies when it comes to leadership and the constitution and bylaws in a local church. But I know of no form of church government that would not allow the pastor to submit his report and recommendations to the elected authority at their regular meetings. As a group, the overseers have the responsibility to set policy and give direction. They are not elected as "yes men" who robotically rubber stamp the pastor's wishes. Then, the rest of the month, those same people change hats and come under the leadership of the pastor and function in a harmonious relationship according to the constitution, bylaws, policy manual, and ministry descriptions. These documents should give a clear picture of the organizational chart and clearly state who is responsible for whom and to whom. All of this requires an attitude of submission one to another on the part of everyone.

Control issues

Gene Wood, in his book titled *Leading Turnaround Churches*, states that "95 percent of all serious problems in the church stem from a power struggle." There are many explanations for this, but the sad part is that not only do people get hurt and churches split, but God is not glorified. Some have described this as the "church boss syndrome." Somehow, over the years, one person becomes the self-appointed leader. Pastors come and pastors go, but the "boss" stays in power. Other times, it is a key family in the church who runs the church and often runs the pastor out of town. There are pastors who have a "benevolent dictator" concept of church leadership, which typically means that people either go along with the pastor's ideas or they leave. None of these scenarios are compatible with an attitude of submission one to another in the fear of God.

Church Discipline

Although church discipline is a lost art in most churches today, it is still a vital part of biblical authority. As I review almost eighteen years of serving as a district superintendent, my biggest surprise is how little local church leaders understand and practice Matthew 18:15-17 and Galatians 6:1. Church leaders need to study the entire subject of church discipline in passages such as Romans 16:17-18; 1 Corinthians 5; 2 Corinthians 2:6-11; 2 Thessalonians 3:14-15; 1 Timothy 5:19-21; 6:3-5; Titus 3:10-11; and Hebrews 3:13.

Discipline is an essential part of all relationships and one of the highest expressions of love. God has designed the church in such a way that leaders willingly watch over our souls and will give an account to God (Hebrews 13:17; 1 Peter 5:2-3). God does this to protect us and expects us to gratefully respond with an attitude of submission to those "who are over us in the Lord." This is one of the many benefits of church membership. In the context of church discipline, church leaders are not responsible to watch over nonmembers. Church discipline is not just the authority to excommunicate, but includes the responsibility to create an atmosphere of encouragement and admonishment so as to avoid the need for excommunication. Discipline should be preventative more than punitive. "No discipline seems pleasant at the time, but painful. Later on, however, it produces a harvest of righteousness and peace for those who have been trained by it" (Hebrews 12:11). The key is an attitude of submission to those in authority that includes a teachable spirit.

Leading by Consensus

This has become much more popular as a leadership style in churches during the past few years. Obviously, there are times when consensus is needed. But there are problems when that becomes the only way to make group decisions. Operating by consensus gives the chairman far too much power and tends to perpetuate the myth that if you don't make a decision now, you are not making a decision. The glaring flaw of "yes men" increases in this environment. And often the result is a superficial sense of unity around the table, but out in the parking lot or around the water cooler at work the next day, dissatisfaction from all sides is expressed.

> Operating by consensus gives the chairman far too much power and tends to perpetuate the myth that if you don't make a decision now, you are not making a decision.

How much better it is to have a full, free, open discussion followed by a call for the vote, without the requirement that it be unanimous. (Requiring a unanimous vote may precipitate another problem—the possibility of one person's vote deciding the outcome.) The vote is taken. Let's say the result is seven in favor and four opposed. Here is where the attitude of submission comes in. The four who voted no, with an attitude of Christ-like submission one to another, submit to the majority and joyfully support the decision as if they had voted for it (assuming it does not violate personal biblical convictions, in which case an appeal would need to be made).

Collective Bargaining in the Workplace

There is (and always will be) a creative tension between management and labor. None of this would be necessary if both obeyed the clear teaching of God's Word. Employers are to provide employees with "what is right and fair, because you know that you also have a Master in heaven" (Colossians 4:1). Employees are to work "with all your heart, as working for the Lord, not for men" (Colossians 3:23). But what should a believer do as an employee when the employer does not do what God says? Start by reading 1 Peter 2:18-21 and "submit yourselves to your masters with all respect, not only to those who are good and considerate, but also to those who are harsh. For it is commendable if a man bears up under the pain of unjust suffering because he is conscious of God." Then, with an attitude of submission, be responsible for making a strong appeal through proper legal channels. Allow the Holy Spirit to lead you through this process and show you how much you need to be involved. He may lead you to quit that job and find a better one with an employer who obeys God.

Husbands and Wives

It is interesting to note that when Paul makes the broad foundational statement of "Submit to one another out of reverence for Christ," the first relationship he writes about is: "Wives, submit to your husbands as to the Lord" (Ephesians 5:21-22). To summarize Ephesians 5:22-33, the husband has two areas of responsibility—to love his wife as Christ loved the church and to lead as head of his wife as Christ leads as the head of the church. The wife also has two areas of responsibility—to submit to her husband and to respect her husband. What do you think would happen to the divorce rate (between forty and fifty percent according to the best current estimates) if these principles were followed? In our culture, many men have copped out of their responsibility to lovingly lead. (Many fathers and mothers also abdicate their leadership roles with their children.) Instead of wives wisely encouraging their husbands to lead and waiting for them to lead, they take on the leadership role out of desperation and self-protection. It seems so radical today, but what would happen if wives practiced this Christ-like attitude of submission "as to the Lord" and experienced the security and freedom that comes from living God's way?

Living in a Godless Nation

The best research by biblical scholars indicates that Paul wrote the letter to the Roman Christians sometime between AD 56–58. Nero was the Roman Emperor from AD 54 to 68. In AD 64, legend has it, the city of Rome burned while Nero fiddled. Christians who refused to worship the emperor were exposed to wild animals and smeared with pitch before being set ablaze in "Nero's circus." Obviously, it takes time for power to be corrupted to that extent. However, it must have been difficult for the church in Rome to hear Paul's words, "Everyone must submit himself to the governing authorities" (Romans 13:1-7). We in America have been spoiled for so many years because God has richly blessed America. However, the more godless we become as a nation, the more committed Christians will need to learn how to live a Christ-like life in a hostile environment.

RESULT: "THEIRS [ALONE] IS THE KINGDOM OF HEAVEN."

When we have genuine humility that can be seen in our response to proper authority, we are blessed and we have the kingdom of heaven. Jesus stated this Beatitude in the present tense. If there is a kingdom, there must be a King. Those who are in this kingdom are subject to the King here and now. This means that when we come into Christ's kingdom by submitting to Him as the King of our lives, we inherit all the blessings of being a child of the King. "To Him who loved us and washed us from our sins in His own blood, and has made us kings and priests to His God and Father, to Him be glory and dominion forever and ever. Amen" (Revelation 1:5-6 NKJV). We enter His kingdom by coming dependently and submissively to Him by faith as a little child (Mark 10:14-15). Jesus also taught that it is hard for a rich man to enter His kingdom, obviously because of his pride, independence, and rebellion (Matthew 19:23). Tragically, people are still saying today what they said in Luke 19:14, "We don't want this man to be our king."

There is an earthly, millennial aspect of this concept of "theirs is the kingdom of heaven" (see Revelation 20). There is also a heavenly, eternal aspect in the new heavens and the new earth as revealed in Revelation 21 and 22. However, Jesus emphasized the present when He said, "Theirs is the kingdom of heaven." We have the kingdom blessings—the promises related to each Beatitude—now. Warren Wiersbe titled his book on the Beatitudes—*Live Like a King*. We who were slaves to our sinful nature and beggars after a crust of bread when it comes to entering God's kingdom can, by the grace of God, live like kings right here and now.

O, God, I pray that each day You will remind me of my absolute dependence upon you for salvation, for spiritual formation, for effective spiritual ministry, and for everyday Christian living. Also, I ask You to work the attitude of submission to proper authority into every area of my life. May my life demonstrate these qualities so those around me will see Christ in me, not my trying to be like Christ. May I have a much fuller picture of who You are; a more accurate picture of myself; a much deeper sense of security; much more freedom in Christ; and a full sense of joy in the kingdom of heaven. Continually show me that Your way really is the best way! Amen.

PERSONAL-REFLECTION QUESTIONS

- What is the hardest part of "submit to one another" for you to joyfully obey?
- What are some ways in which you tend to put yourself down?
- Specifically, where do you struggle with the issue of accepting yourself as God made you?
- How do you see yourself as a "bond slave" of Christ?
- How are you doing with the "personal disciplines" suggestions?

GROUP-DISCUSSION QUESTIONS

- What are some of the common misunderstandings regarding submission, and how can we correct them?
- How can we prevent "control issues" in the church?
- When do we appeal to authority, and when do we remain silent?
- How can we do better when it comes to "by love, serve one another"?
- How well are we doing as a group/church when it comes to equipping others—making disciples?

4

The Blessedness of Being Mournful!

Blessed are those who mourn, for they will be comforted. (Matthew 5:4)

Webster's Dictionary defines paradox as "a statement that is seemingly contradictory or opposed to common sense and yet is perhaps true." The Bible contains many paradoxical truths such as:

- The way down is the way up.
- To be low is to be high.
- The broken heart is the healed heart.
- The contrite spirit is the rejoicing spirit.
- The repenting soul is the victorious soul.
- To lose your life is to save it.
- To have nothing is to possess all things.
- To bear the cross is to wear the crown.
- To give is to receive.
- The valley is the place of vision.

This Beatitude is a prime example of a paradox. It seems to be saying, "Happy are the unhappy." When someone says, "Complete this sentence: Happiness is . . ." how many people would include "mourning" in their answer?

When Jesus taught "Blessed are those who mourn," He revealed how countercultural His kingdom really is. This Beatitude is a far cry from the mind-set of our day. Today, the thinking is: we have to be tough (not tender) in order to get what we want and be happy. We live in a pleasure-mad world. Amusement, entertainment, and thrill-seeking are designed to bring happiness and avoid mourning. People want to laugh, but never cry. They grumble and complain when hard times come. Pain is seen as an enemy, not a friend. We naturally do everything possible to circumvent suffering and sorrow. However, Jesus turned these thought-patterns upside down.

The Bible has a lot to say about mourning, weeping, sorrowing, and suffering. The preacher in Ecclesiastes wrote: "It is better to go to a house of mourning than to go to a house of feasting, for death is the destiny of every man; the living should take this to heart. Sorrow is better than laughter, because a sad face is good for the heart. The heart of the wise is in the house of mourning, but the heart of fools is in the house of pleasure" (7:2-4). The fact that there are nine different Greek words used in the New Testament to describe the different experiences of mourning is clear evidence that this is a massive subject. The story of humankind is a story of tears and grief and trouble. This is the human experience. And it is only going to get worse. In Matthew 24, where Jesus gives us a picture of a buildup of troubling events just prior to His second coming, He concludes by saying, "But all this is only the first of the birth pains, with more to come" (Matthew 24:8 NLT). We, as believers in Jesus Christ, are to live a life in bold contrast to the thinking of the world, while understanding that only those who mourn will be comforted.

APPROPRIATE, NORMAL, HEALTHY MOURNING, WEEPING, AND SORROWING

There are many forms of and reasons for appropriate, normal, healthy mourning. When something happens that seems tragic to us, it is appropriate to weep. Ecclesiastes 3 says "There is a time for everything . . . a time to weep and a time to laugh." Here are some examples:

Mourning when we experience a loss. This type of mourning could be from any of the following: financial loss, job loss, loss of priceless possessions, loss of good health, loss of freedom, or the death of a loved one. Abraham justifiably mourned when Sarah died (Genesis 23:2). Rather than being a sign of weakness to cry at funerals, it is normal and healthy. Hezekiah prayed with tears when he became sick; when God saw his tears, He healed him (2 Kings 20:5). Job "poured out tears to God" when he lost everything (Job 16:20). Ecclesiastes 4:1-3 is about "tears of the oppressed." The father of a boy with an evil spirit came to Jesus for healing and "cried out and said with tears, 'Lord, I believe; help my unbelief!'" (Mark 9:24 NKJV)

Mourning when we intercede for others. There are many biblical illustrations that reveal the heart of an earnest intercessor. Loving and caring for someone enough to cry out to God with tears is the appropriate response when a friend is in trouble.

Mourning when we are lonely and discouraged. The ability to weep as we go through valleys in life is a gift from God to release the sorrow of our hearts. How many times do you read about crying like this in the Psalms? Paul wrote to young Timothy, "I constantly remember you in my prayers. Recalling your tears, I long to see you, so that I may be filled with joy" (2 Timothy 1:4). I picture Timothy as a rather melancholy pastor who was left alone in Ephesus when Paul went on to Macedonia. He wept as a lot of pastors do. Can you imagine how encouraged Timothy was when he heard that Paul was constantly praying for him and wanted to see him because he, Timothy, would fill Paul with joy?

Mourning when we see pending doom coming to others. After all the ways that King Saul had disobeyed God and even after Samuel knew that God had taken the kingdom away from him, Samuel still "mourned for him" (1 Samuel 15:35). Esther "pleaded with the king, falling at his feet and weeping . . . to put an end to the evil plan of Haman . . . against the Jews" (Esther 8:3). Jeremiah is known as the "weeping prophet." He understood the judgment about to come upon God's chosen people. Instead of gloating, he wept. He prayed, "I mourn, and horror grips me. Is there no balm in Gilead? Is there no physician there? Why then is there no healing for the wound of my people? Oh, that my head were a spring of water and my eyes a fountain of tears! I would weep day and night for the slain of my people" (Jeremiah 8:21–9:1). Think of all the problems that Paul had to deal with in the Corinthian church. When others would have been disgusted, he wrote to them "out of great distress and anguish of heart and with many tears, not to grieve you but to let you know the depth of my love for you" (2 Corinthians 2:4). How good it would be for people to weep like this over the unrighteousness in our nation and the apostasy in our churches rather than stand on the sidelines with their self-righteous, pharisaical "flowing robes" around them (Mark 12:38).

Mourn when others are weeping. In the church, we "mourn with those who mourn" (Romans 12:15). That is the ultimate expression of compassion and empathy. People outside of the church need to see this depth of unity when they look at the church.

Mourn when there are unmet spiritual desires. The psalmist wrote, "As the deer pants for streams of water, so my soul pants for you, O God. My soul thirsts for God, for the living God. When can I go and meet with God? My tears have been my food day and night" (Psalm 42:1-3). Regardless of where we are in our spiritual journey, there are times when our quest for God brings us to tears. Growing older in Christ does not mean we will cry less; it may mean we will cry more. In fact, spiritual maturity redefines the things that make us cry.

INAPPROPRIATE, ABNORMAL, UNHEALTHY MOURNING, WEEPING, AND SORROWING

Not all tears are normal and healthy. Some are destructive and have a negative effect. Sometimes people mourn for the wrong reasons. Here are some examples:

Remorseful tears. "When Judas, who had betrayed him, saw that Jesus was condemned, he was seized with remorse and returned the thirty silver coins" (Matthew 27:3). He was sorry, he openly acknowledged his sin, he said, "I have sinned . . . for I have betrayed innocent blood" (27:4); and he made restitution by returning the thirty silver coins (27:3). Judas took all those steps toward true repentance, yet he "went away and hanged himself" (27:5). Study the contrast between Judas and Peter to understand the difference between godly sorrow and remorseful tears. Peter denied his Lord, but when he heard the rooster crow, he "went out and wept bitterly." He was restored and became the leader in the early church. "The same sun that melts butter hardens clay." Peter was the "butter" and Judas the "clay."

Hypocritical tears. King Saul's "repentance" was phony. Although he looked like a mourner on the outside, he had a disobedient heart. (Even though I can find no verse that says Saul wept, I understand that in the Old Testament, "repenting" included penitence, sorrowing, mourning, and tears.) When Samuel confronted Saul on several occasions, instead of truly repenting, he made excuses rather than admitting his sin. Even when he did acknowledge his sin, there was no shame since he wanted Samuel to go with him and honor him before the elders in order to preserve his reputation (1 Samuel 15:30). There was nothing genuine about Saul's mourning.

Bitter tears. When God did not accept Cain's offering, he was "very angry, and his face was downcast" (Genesis 4:5). Then Cain murdered his brother Abel. God pronounced a curse on Cain and drove him from that part of the earth. Again, although I don't see the word "tears" in the text, it is easy for me to imagine tears flowing when he said to God, "My punishment is more than I can bear" (Genesis 4:13). Here is a bitter, angry man more troubled by his punishment than by the fact that he had killed his brother. "So Cain went out from the LORD's presence and lived in the land of Nod, east of Eden" (Genesis 4:16), which only demonstrated his lack of genuine sorrow for sin.

Covetous tears. A story in 1 Kings 21 serves as a good example of this kind of "mourning." Ahab, king of Samaria, coveted the vineyard that belonged to Naboth the Jezreelite. Naboth refused to give it to him because it was a family heirloom passed down from generation to generation. So Ahab became "sullen" and "lay on his bed sulking and refused to eat." He pouted because he could not get his way. Have you ever known someone who cried as a means to get what he or she wanted? That is selfish "mourning." It is sorrowing that leads to depression when the covetousness is not fulfilled. It is abnormal and unhealthy. (Parents, read the rest of the story and learn to never give in to pouting tears.)

Unrelieved tears. Absalom, the son of King David, was a wicked, proud, self-centered man. He hated his father and tried to dethrone him. The coup failed. King David won, and Absalom finally died a tragic death (2 Samuel 18). Couriers brought the news to David. "The king was shaken. He went up to the room over the gateway and wept. As he went, he said: 'O my son Absalom! My son, my son Absalom! If only I had died instead of you—O Absalom, my son, my son!'" (18:33). At that moment, David no doubt remembered his own words to Nathan, the prophet who confronted him regarding his sin with Bathsheba. David's response to the story Nathan told him was, "The man who did this deserves to die! He must pay for that lamb four times over, because he did such a thing and had no pity.' Then Nathan said to David, 'You are the man!'" (2 Samuel 12:6-7). Look at the four things that subsequently happened to David. The baby from that union died. His daughter Tamar was violated incestuously. His son Amnon was killed, and now Absalom is dead prematurely. David could not stop crying. He had said, "My sin is always before me" (Psalm 51:3), but we must also know that our sins are covered by the blood of Christ. However, some people continuously sorrow in an abnormal way in an effort to atone for their sins. It is one thing to grieve, but there is an abnormal, unhealthy preoccupation with mourning that becomes self-centered and leads to a kind of paranoia. When we experience that dark night of mourning, we must remember that "joy comes in the morning." The Christian's life is not to be characterized by a morose, glum, sullen, forlorn disposition. Jesus did not say, "Blessed are the gloomy Christians." Paul wrote about being "sorrowful yet always rejoicing" (2 Corinthians 2:10). There is a huge difference between weeping and being weepy. Continuous mourning is abnormal and unhealthy.

Worldly tears. This paragraph includes a large assortment of tears—from "crocodile tears" to wallowing in self-pity to any type of mourning that is only external. It includes self-induced weeping and self-inflicted grief. Not all mourners will be comforted. There is a "worldly sorrow [that] brings death" (2 Corinthians 7:10). When people mourn without experiencing the "fruit of repentance," that mourning is detrimental to their spiritual lives. It simply adds to the sense of despair and depression. Without coming to Christ with godly sorrow for sin, there is no answer, no hope, and no cleansing cure for sin.

Hellish tears. According to the Scriptures, hell is a place where there is "weeping and gnashing of teeth" (Matthew 8:12). I can't begin to imagine that scene. It is the most horrific, never-ending existence. On the other hand, heaven is a place where God "will wipe every tear from their eyes" (Revelation 21:4). We have every reason to believe every word of the divinely inspired Word of God—including words about heaven and hell. Why would anyone choose to endure mourning, weeping, and sorrowing in hell forever?

GODLY MOURNING, WEEPING, AND SORROWING

Paul wrote to the Corinthian believers, "Now I am happy, not because you were made sorry, but because your sorrow led you to repentance. For you became sorrowful as God intended and so were not harmed in any way by us. Godly sorrow brings repentance that leads to salvation, and leaves no regret" (2 Corinthians 7:9-10). The word for "mourn" in Matthew 5:4 is the strongest and most intense of nine words in the original language that are translated into English as "mourn," "sorrow," "weep," etc. It is typically reserved for experiences of death—physical and spiritual. (Study verses such as Matthew 9:15; Mark 16:10; 1 Corinthians 5:2; 2 Corinthians 12:21; James 4:9 where the Greek word "pentheo" [mourn] is found.) It is grieving which is so profound that it takes possession of our whole being in ways that cannot be concealed. It is the kind of passionate lamenting that we see in the book of Lamentations and in many of the Psalms.

Again, it is helpful to learn what something is by learning what it is not. Hard-heartedness is the extreme opposite of the mind-set that results in the activity of mourning. In the middle of Paul's description of godless natural affection in the last days, he mentions "without love" or hard-heartedness (2 Timothy 3:3, KJV – also referred to as "inordinate affection" in Colossians 3:5 KJV). It is a fearful thing to have a hard heart. Like people who are deaf and don't know what sounds they are missing, hard-hearted people are so calloused and insensitive that they don't even realize it. That's why the Bible warns, "Do not harden your hearts" (Hebrews 4:7).

It is a serious thing to resist God's efforts when He brings testing and discipline into our lives with the intention of producing a broken and contrite heart. That is why Jeremiah prayed, "O LORD, do not your eyes look for truth? You struck them, but they felt no pain; you crushed them, but they refused correction. They made their faces harder than stone and refused to repent" (Jeremiah 5:3). This is not about "broken people" as a medical doctor or psychiatrist would use that phrase. Rather, it is about an internal broken and contrite spirit that is spiritually healthy. A stony heart cannot mourn. Ezekiel also used the metaphor of a stony heart when he wrote, "I [God] will give you a new heart and put a new spirit in you; I will remove from you your heart of stone and give you a heart of flesh" (Ezekiel 36:26).

> It is a serious thing to resist God's efforts when He brings testing and discipline into our lives with the intention of producing a broken and contrite heart.

There are many terrifying consequences of hardening our hearts against God. The Bible says, "He who hardens his heart falls into trouble" (Proverbs 28:14). "Because of your stubbornness and your unrepentant heart, you are storing up wrath against yourself for the day of God's wrath, when his righteous judgment will be revealed" (Romans 2:5). "They are darkened in their understanding and separated from the life of God because of the ignorance that is in them due to the hardening of their hearts" (Ephesians 4:18). Jesus explained to the Pharisees why Moses permitted divorce when He said, "It was because your hearts were hard that Moses wrote you this law" (Mark 10:2-12). Pharaoh persisted in resisting God until God hardened his heart (Exodus 4:21; 10:20). Hardness of heart can take us beyond hope, like Esau who sold his birthright. "Afterward, as you know, when he wanted to inherit this blessing, he was rejected. He could bring about no change of mind, though he sought the blessing with tears" (Hebrews 12:17).

The key to this Beatitude is found in being tender-hearted. "You do not delight in sacrifice, or I would bring it; you do not take pleasure in burnt offerings. The sacrifices of God are a broken spirit; a broken and contrite heart, O God, you will not despise" (Psalm 51:16-17). Broken can also be rendered crushed, broken in pieces, torn, and brought to birth. Contrite means being collapsed physically or mentally. These two words describe a soul in devastated brokenness that manifests itself in mourning, weeping, and sorrowing.

The seasons of crushing brokenness we all endure are like birth pangs. In Matthew 7:14, Jesus talked about a narrow way that leads to life. The word narrow means "to suffer tribulation" and "pressure." Like a baby coming through the narrow way of the birth canal, the pressures of our sorrows are actually meant to bring our hearts to birth, to life, by the power of God's grace. In Galatians 4:19, Paul wrote, "My dear children, for whom I am again in the pains of childbirth until Christ is formed in you." That word "pains" is from the root word meaning "to lament and mourn." Jesus used the same metaphor of laboring in childbirth to describe the weeping and lamentation His disciples would endure upon His death (John 16:20-21). Many of the Psalms also give us an intimate glimpse into the tearful prayers of the brokenhearted.

Mark Buchanan wrote in his book *Your God is too Safe*: "Brokenness molds our character closer to the character of God more than anything else. To experience defeat, disappointment, loss—the raw ingredients of brokenness—moves us closer to being like God than victory and gain and fulfillment ever can." This is how our hearts are tenderized. We have no right to expect that God will do anything with our lives until we are broken and contrite before Him. Our disappointments (which God uses to bring about this tenderness in us) are God's appointments. What we think of as tragedies may be blessings in disguise. People who have been affected the most by pain and suffering are often the most effective. A. W. Tozer said, "God will only use us greatly when we have been hurt deeply." This concept of brokenness is one of the most important and misunderstood spiritual dynamics in the Word of God.

LET'S LOOK AT JESUS

Jesus is God in bodily form. When most of us think of God, the last thing we consider is His weeping in brokenness. This is because we hold an incomplete and distorted view of the ways of God in suffering.

Jesus—God incarnate—came to earth where He was "a man of sorrows, and familiar with suffering" (Isaiah 53:3). "During the days of Jesus' life on earth, he offered up prayers and petitions with loud cries and tears to the one who could save him from death, and he was heard because of his reverent submission. Although he was a son, he learned obedience from what he suffered" (Hebrews 5:7-8).

"Jesus wept" when His close friend, Lazarus, died (John 11:35). Later, "as he approached Jerusalem and saw the city, he wept over it and said, 'If you, even you, had only known on this day what would bring you peace—but now it is hidden from your eyes'" (Luke 19:41). Some thought that Jesus was Jeremiah, the weeping prophet (Matthew 16:14). There is no record of Jesus laughing. I believe He smiled and had a cheerful heart which "is good medicine" (Proverbs 17:22). He attended weddings and other festive occasions, but overall there was seriousness about His life on earth. The joy He talked about and exemplified was not external or superficial. Because of the things He suffered, there was sensitivity in His demeanor and tenderness in His eyes. I have tried to picture in my mind that scene where, after Peter had denied the Lord three times and the rooster crowed, "the Lord turned and looked at Peter" (Luke 22:61 NLT). I believe there was hurt, sadness, and disappointment, but also a soft tenderness in the eyes of Jesus as He looked at Peter.

The night in which Jesus was betrayed, He took Peter, James, and John further into the garden of Gethsemane and said to them, "My soul is overwhelmed with sorrow to the point of death. . . . Stay here and keep watch" (Mark 14:34). Jesus "withdrew about a stone's throw beyond them. . . . And being in anguish, he prayed more earnestly, and his sweat was like drops of blood falling to the ground" (Luke 22:41-44). On the cross, "He took up our infirmities and carried our sorrows, yet we considered him stricken by God, smitten by him, and afflicted. But he was pierced for our transgressions, he was crushed for our iniquities; the punishment that brought us peace was upon him, and by his wounds we are healed" (Isaiah 53:4-5).

There is no way we will ever (not even in eternity) fully know what Christ experienced in those dark hours on the cross. Native Americans have a saying: "Before we can truly understand another person, we must walk a mile in their moccasins. Before we can walk in another person's moccasins, we must first take off our own." In the later years of my pastoral ministry, I felt very close to my district superintendent. He graciously invited me to be with him in some very difficult and pressure-packed situations. But it was not until I was elected to serve as a district superintendent myself that I understood what it meant to "face daily the pressure of my concern for all the churches" (2 Corinthians 11:28). There are some things you must experience in order to understand. Since we will never take Jesus' place on the cross as He took our place, we will never know the extent of His mourning! But in Christ, we have the perfect example of how to mourn, weep, and experience sorrow.

MOURNING BECAUSE OF OUR OWN SINS

James 4:6-10 says, "God opposes the proud but gives grace to the humble. Submit yourselves, then, to God. Resist the devil, and he will flee from you. Come near to God and he will come near to you. Wash your hands, you sinners, and purify your hearts, you double-minded. Grieve, mourn and wail. Change your laughter to mourning and your joy to gloom. Humble yourselves before the Lord, and he will lift you up." Humility and mourning go together. Until we acknowledge our spiritual poverty we cannot truly mourn over sin. If we do not mourn over sin, we only prove that we are ignorant of our dire spiritual condition and how much our sins have grieved God.

Part of the gospel story is that we must recognize our utter dependence upon the work of Christ on the cross for our salvation. Another part of the salvation experience is weeping and mourning over the grief our sinfulness brought to the heart of God. Genuine conversion must involve all three aspects of our personhood—intellect, emotion, and will. God is offended by a stiff neck, haughty eyes, and an unteachable spirit. But the good news of the gospel is that God will never despise a broken and contrite heart (Psalm 51:17). He never rejects a person who comes to Him with the attitude of brokenness.

> Genuine conversion must involve all three aspects of our personhood—intellect, emotion, and will.

When we see our own spiritual poverty, we have at least four options: 1. Deny it. 2. Admit it and try to fix things ourselves. 3. Admit our need and give up in despair. 4. Admit it and turn to God with a sorrow that leads to repentance. Repentance is not merely a decision; it is a fruit of godly sorrow. "Godly sorrow brings repentance that leads to salvation" (2 Corinthians 7:10). Before there is salvation there must be repentance. Before there is repentance there must be godly sorrow. True repentance is a rending of the heart. It is the fruit of the brokenness of mourning, not merely regret for sin. If we do not mourn deeply over our sin, we will not truly repent. "'Even now,' declares the LORD, 'return to me with all your heart, with fasting and weeping and mourning.' Rend your heart and not your garments. Return to the LORD your God, for he is gracious and compassionate, slow to anger and abounding in love, and he relents from sending calamity" (Joel 2:12-13).

Oswald Chambers wrote, "The foundation of Christianity is repentance. Strictly speaking, a person cannot repent when he chooses—repentance is a gift of God." The Puritans prayed for "the gift of tears." They actually called themselves "repenters" rather than Christians. I understand that even today believers in Russia don't ask people when they were saved or when they became a Christian. Instead, they ask, "When did you repent? Have you repented?" *The Book of Common Prayer* includes prayers like this: "Almighty and everlasting God, who hatest nothing that thou hast made, and dost forgive the sins of all those who are penitent; Create and make in us new and contrite hearts, that we, worthily lamenting our sins, and acknowledging our wretchedness, may obtain of thee, the God of all mercy, perfect remission and forgiveness; through Jesus Christ our Lord. Amen."

I remember the days when we had an altar in the front of our meeting places where people would kneel and weep their way through to God. In past generations that was called "the mourners' bench." For the most part, the church today lives in a world of dry-eyed confession of sin, a mere decision of the will without the deep conviction birthed in godly sorrow for sin. "Blessed are those who mourn" includes a godly sorrow for sin that results in God's forgiveness, which is the greatest of all comforts. "Blessed are they whose transgressions are forgiven, whose sins are covered. Blessed is the man whose sin the Lord will never count against him" (Romans 4:7-8).

MOURNING BECAUSE OF THE SINS OF OTHERS

In addition to the biblical illustrations already used, David said, "Rivers of tears gush from my eyes because people disobey your instructions" (Psalm 119:136 NLT). Micah wept in prayer for God's people (Micah 1:8-9). Nehemiah, Daniel, and Joel all wept over the sins of others. Jeremiah said, "This is why I weep and my eyes overflow with tears. . . . My children are destitute because the enemy has prevailed" (Lamentations 1:16). God said to Ezekiel, "Son of man, groan before the people! Groan before them with bitter anguish and a broken heart. When they ask why you are groaning, tell them, 'I groan because of the terrifying news I have heard. When it comes true, the boldest heart will melt with fear; all strength will disappear. Every spirit will faint; strong knees will become as weak as water. And the Sovereign LORD says: It is coming! It's on its way!'" (Ezekiel 21:6-7 NLT).

I often wondered why God spared Lot. Then I read 2 Peter 2:7-8 where God calls Lot a "righteous man" who was "distressed" and "tormented [anguished, afflicted, vexed, troubled, crushed, grieved, burdened] in his righteous soul by the lawless deeds he saw and heard." Jesus was described as "being grieved by the hardness of their hearts" (Mark 3:5, NKJV). Paul sets a good example when he writes, "As I have often told you before and now say again even with tears, many live as enemies of the cross of Christ" (Philippians 3:18). He told the Corinthians, "You are proud! Shouldn't you rather have been filled with grief and have put out of your fellowship the man who did this?" (1 Corinthians 5:2). Mourning is the proper atmosphere for church discipline. People in the Corinthian church were proud of their open-mindedness and pluralistic ideas when they should have been mourning over the sins of others. God gives us discernment to see these things, not to criticize or gossip or ignore, but to pray—with tears. This mourning should be recognized as something beyond any human ability to do. This is a God-thing which He works in our lives by His Holy Spirit.

MOURNING IN EVERYDAY LIFE

This attitude of brokenness and tenderheartedness, rather than being a one-time experience, is a continuous mind-set. The goal is not to mourn and weep and experience sorrow every minute of every day. Rather, it is to welcome experiences that God allows to come into our lives that cause us to mourn, and see them result in making us broken and tender-hearted before God. Hardness is our natural default mode because of our bent toward self-sufficiency and independence. It takes mourning and weeping and sorrowing to change that. God has designed this grieving and those tears to release that pain and to be part of a healing process. When pain is pent up inside, it can poison the mental and emotional and spiritual system. Conversely, mourning leads to the cleansing of that poison.

Beyond this natural, positive effect of mourning, there is a deep, spiritual result that is part of God's work in conforming us to the image of His Son. Just as grapes are crushed to make wine and grain is ground to make bread, so a broken and contrite heart is to be the result of difficult experiences. Godly sorrowing over our sin brings repentance, which in turn brings forgiveness and spiritual healing. God's careful use of ongoing events that cause us to mourn as believers brings a tenderness and sensitivity that makes us more like Jesus. These events are not always tragic and devastating. Suffering comes in all sizes and shapes. Sometimes those events may result in our sinning again so that we need to repeat the process of godly sorrow leading to repentance and resulting in God's forgiveness. Thus, tenderheartedness is both a means to an end and, at the same time, a desired end.

Charles Spurgeon wrote: "Heart-rending is divinely wrought and solemnly felt. It is a secret grief which is personally experienced, not in mere form, but as a deep, soul moving work of the Holy Spirit upon the inmost heart of each believer. It is not a matter to be merely talked of and believed in, but keenly and sensitively felt in every living child of the living God. It is powerfully humiliating, and completely sin-purging; but then it is sweetly preparative for those gracious consolations which proud, unhumbled spirits are unable to receive; and it is distinctly discriminating, for it belongs to the elect of God and to them alone."

TEARS

Physically, tears are a good thing. Tears help us see. Basal tears constantly lubricate our eyeballs and eyelids. No lubrication—no eyesight. Tears also kill bacteria and remove toxins. Tears lower stress and release pent-up feelings.

Someone has described tears as "emotional perspiration." Perhaps it helps us understand this subject to think about the pores of our skin being open. When skin is covered with dirt or makeup and no soap and water or exfoliating gel are applied, the skin becomes rough and unhealthy.

Spiritually, tears do the same things for the soul. God wants the pores of our spiritual being to be open and vulnerable. As people can feel cleansed emotionally after a good cry, so the person who mourns and weeps with a godly sorrow that leads to repentance will experience the cleansing that God has promised (1 John 1:9). Our tears are precious and valuable to God. David wrote; "You keep track of all my sorrows. You have collected all my tears in your bottle. You have recorded each one in your book" (Psalm 56:8 NLT). We need to value tears as God does.

Tears are the one language we all understand. You may have noticed that I have used the words "mourning", "weeping" and "sorrowing" synonymously and interchangeably. This is scriptural. (See Zechariah 12:10-11, for example.) The question is: Can you mourn without tears? The answer is not as easy as it may appear for several reasons.

First, there are different layers or levels of mourning as indicated by the fact that nine different Greek words are used in the New Testament to describe this experience. It is one thing to mourn at the funeral of a friend. It is another thing to mourn when a family member dies. But when death separates the exclusive attachment of a married couple, the surviving spouse experiences a much deeper mourning. It is important for us to understand that not all levels of mourning always generate tears for everyone every time.

Second, there are different personalities and temperaments given to us by God. Some people are more stoic than others. Some are more easily given to emotional expressions than others. Tears may come in different amounts and for different durations. Just because tears flow more easily for some does not prove they are more spiritually mature. Ultimately, this Beatitude is teaching that we should never steel ourselves against mourning by suppressing the flow of tears. Such behavior can lead to hardness of heart. It is not unmanly to cry. Jesus wept and He was—and is—a man's man.

Third, there are different motivations for crying. Some people will cry crocodile tears to impress people with their supposed tenderness. Some people cry at the "drop of a hat." Others cry as a means of getting what they want. Still others cry to make it appear as if they are mourning. That reminds me of a "spring thaw" in upstate New York where I lived through eleven winters. On the surface, there was a soft, gooey, layer of mud. But, underneath, there was hard, frozen tundra.

The word Jesus used in the Sermon on the Mount for mourn means the deepest and most intense kind of mourning with a lamenting so passionate that it takes possession of our whole being and cannot be concealed. Therefore, I believe this level of mourning will manifest itself in tears as an essential expression of humility and brokenness.

THE WORD OF GOD

God wants the seed of His Word planted where the conviction of His Holy Spirit has brought brokenness, where the fallow ground has been plowed and then watered with the tears of repentance. In Revelation 5:4, John writes, "I wept and wept because no one was found who was worthy to open the scroll or look inside." Could it be that through his tears John saw the one who was worthy to open the sealed book? How many saints have tear-stained Bibles where their tears enabled them to see deeply into divine truth? John Bunyan was imprisoned for twelve years because he refused to promise never to preach the gospel again. His imprisonment caused him great suffering, especially because of the hardship it brought to his already needy family. He wrote in *Grace Abounding to Sinners*, "I never had in all my life so great an inlet into the Word of God as now [in prison]. The Scriptures that I saw nothing in before are made in this place to shine upon me. . . . I have seen things here that I am persuaded I shall never be able to express." As Oswald Chambers has written so wisely, "The Bible was written in tears and to tears it yields its treasures." Just as tears enable us to see physically, so tears that are the result of this kind of mourning enable us to see deeply into the Word of God.

PRAYER

Charles Spurgeon preached, "No prayer will ever prevail with God more surely than a liquid petition, which, being distilled from the heart, trickles from the eye, and waters the cheek." In addition to those we have already mentioned who prayed with tears, we have the example of Hannah who "wept much and prayed to the LORD" (1 Samuel 1:10). God gave her a son in answer to prevailing prayer. Oswald Chambers wrote of such prayers: "Prayer is the falling of a tear. God regards not high looks and lofty words; He cares not for the pomp and pageantry of kings; He listens not to the swell of martial music; He regards not the triumph and pride of man; but wherever there is a heart big with sorrow, or a lip quivering with agony, or a deep groan, or a penitential sigh, the heart of Jehovah is open; He marks it down in the registry of His memory; He puts our prayers, like rose leaves, between the pages of His book of remembrance, and when the volume is opened at last, there shall be a precious fragrance springing up therefrom." This is part of the great value of mourning.

LISTENING

Our culture suffers from an overload of apathy and hardness. This is clearly seen in the superficiality and triteness of our conversation. There is so little "spirit to spirit" communication, even among Christians. Our scientific, technological generation demands empirical proof, even when it comes to spiritual reality. This hardness of heart means that the pores of our spiritual being are clogged, causing us to slip deeper into a pit of isolation and despair. Rather than being vulnerable and broken, we build walls around us to protect ourselves; as a result we really don't know how to listen. Only when we are tenderhearted as a result of godly mourning can we really empathize with others and show compassion to them.

Too many people underestimate the value and power of listening. God gave us two ears and one mouth for a reason. We need to get beyond typical conversations. We need to listen with our spiritual ears open, hearing and understanding the spirit beneath the words spoken. Listen with the heart and mind still and the mouth shut. Listen with a compassionate heart that cares deeply about others. Wait patiently, quietly, and prayerfully through times of silence and allow the Holy Spirit to do His transforming work. Recognize these times as "divine appointments" allowing us to be broken vessels that God can use. This kind of listening can be possible only through godly mourning.

THEY [ALONE] WILL BE COMFORTED

This is the promise of God. It is found throughout Scripture. "Weeping may endure for a night, but joy comes in the morning" (Psalm 30:5 NKJV). "You turned my wailing into dancing; you removed my sackcloth and clothed me with joy, that my heart may sing to you and not be silent. O LORD my God, I will give you thanks forever" (Psalm 30:11-12). Isaiah writes in 61:2-3, "To proclaim the year of the LORD's favor and the day of vengeance of our God, to comfort all who mourn, and provide for those who grieve in Zion—to bestow on them a crown of beauty instead of ashes, the oil of gladness instead of mourning, and a garment of praise instead of a spirit of despair. They will be called oaks of righteousness, a planting of the LORD for the display of his splendor."

There is a very relevant example of pain and sorrow turning into joy that every mother understands—and men don't. "A woman, when she is in labor, has sorrow because her hour has come; but as soon as she has given birth to the child, she no longer remembers the anguish, for joy that a human being has been born into the world" (John 16:21 NKJV).

This promised comfort is related to the promise of the coming of the Comforter—

the Holy Spirit who dwells within us. Obviously, we experience this comfort when we know God's cleansing and forgiveness, as we allow godly sorrow to bring us to repentance that brings salvation. This is the most comforting experience we can have in our entire life. We also know His comfort as we allow our mourning to produce in us a tender heart and a sensitive spirit that is like the heart of Jesus. It is comforting to know that hardness of heart is gone and the hindrances to a broken heart removed so we can hear Him whisper, "This is the way, walk in it." So many Christians know the broad strokes of biblical commandments, but struggle when it comes to knowing the will of God where Scripture is silent. Living this Beatitude will enable us to know His specific will for us each day. The ultimate comfort, of course, is when we get to heaven where "[God] will wipe away every tear from their eyes" (Revelation 21:4). Remember, comfort does not come from the mourning, but from the One who is "the God of all comfort" (2 Corinthians 1:3).

> So many Christians know the broad strokes of biblical commandments, but struggle when it comes to knowing the will of God where Scripture is silent.

O God, I pray that the trials You allow into my life will lead to godly mourning that, in turn, will produce in me a tender heart and a sensitive spirit. Thank you for the gift of those holy moments when You are at work in me. By Your grace, give to me the gift of tears that reflect a deep, inner brokenness before You. Grant to me the ability to weep deeply over my own sins and the sins of others that so deeply grieve You. Give to me the joy of my salvation that comes after genuine repentance. Amen.

PERSONAL-REFLECTION QUESTIONS

- Review your conversion experience. How would you describe your godly sorrow for sin that led you to repentance?
- How easy is it for your tears to flow?
- How have you experienced God's comfort?
- How would you describe the last time you felt your heart breaking for someone else?
- How are you doing when it comes to listening with a tender heart?

GROUP-DISCUSSION QUESTIONS

- What are some common, practical, everyday things that cause and/or reveal hardness of heart?
- What is one new thing you learned about mourning in this chapter?
- What are some indicators of "hardness of heart" in our culture?
- How do you see "brokenness" related to "humility"?
- How does the comforting ministry of the Holy Spirit tie into mourning?

5

The Blessedness of Being Meek!

Blessed are the meek, for they will inherit the earth. (Matthew 5:5)

L et's go back to that scene on the mountainside where the Beatitudes were delivered. There is a crowd of people—presumably, mostly Jewish. For centuries they had been looking for the Messiah. In the year 63 BC, Pompey had Palestine annexed into the Roman Empire. This brought an end to the Jewish independence that was gained by the Maccabean Revolution (167 BC). This annexation only heightened the desire for their Messiah who, they hoped, would deliver them from this oppression. Some Jews, called Zealots (Simon, the Zealot, one of Jesus' disciples, was one of them), believed the Messiah would start a revolutionary war and gain back their independence both politically and militarily. The Jewish religious leaders were hoping for a religious movement led by the Messiah that would deliver them from the tyranny of Rome. However, there was also a remnant of godly people such as Simeon and Anna who turned this anticipation of the Messiah into praying that God would send the Messiah (read Luke 2:25-38).

The Old Testament includes a number of prophecies that tell of the coming Messiah. They teach that He is to come as a "suffering Servant" and a "conquering King." The Jewish people in Jesus' day didn't understand this dual role. Even after the resurrection, His disciples still didn't get it. They said, "Lord, are you at this time going to restore the kingdom to Israel?" (Acts 1:6) From our vantage point almost 2000 years later, we understand it is like looking at a mountain range from a distance. We see two mountain peaks—one behind the other. They appear to be together as part of the same mountain. But when we fly over the area, we see they are two separate peaks with acres of valley in between. We now know there are more than 2,000 years between the first coming of the Messiah as the "suffering Servant" and His second coming as the "conquering King."

Back to the Beatitudes and Matthew 5:5. The crowd of people that day was looking for a deliverer. False messiahs had come and gone. However, this time it seemed different. Angels announced this Messiah's birth, magi from the East miraculously found their way to Bethlehem to worship Him, and other supernatural events surrounded His early life. Now, some thirty years later, Jesus was introduced by John the Baptist who was preaching that the kingdom of heaven is near. According to Luke 3:15, "The people were waiting expectantly and were all wondering in their hearts if John might possibly be the Christ [Messiah]." John knew his role and made it clear that Jesus, not he, was the Messiah.

Jesus began His ministry after forty days in the desert and being tempted by the devil. People saw Him heal the sick, raise the dead, and do many other miraculous things to demonstrate that He was the Messiah. Jesus said, "The time has come. . . . The kingdom of God is near. Repent and believe the good news!" (Mark 1:15). Now, on the side of the mountain with a great crowd of people, He is declaring the "Magna Carta" of His kingdom. He begins by saying the citizens in this kingdom are blessed and to be envied. They are humble, brokenhearted, and contrite in spirit—not proud, not self-sufficient, not self-ruled, and not hard-hearted. Next He says, "Blessed are the meek, for they will inherit the earth." But the crowd must have been wondering: How can the Roman government be overthrown if the Jewish people don't assert themselves?

This message was not what they expected. It was absolutely foreign to their thinking. Yet, it was a direct quote from Psalm 37:11. In all of Jesus' teaching He had very little, if anything, to say about the Roman Empire and a lot to say about the Jews, especially their leaders. He thoroughly exasperated the Zealots who wanted the violent overthrow of the Roman domination. When He pointed out the hypocrisy of the religious leaders, they set out to kill Him. This entire scenario is the reason, in part, why the preaching of the cross is a stumbling block to the Jews (1 Corinthians 1:23).

However, Jesus clarified the issue later when He said, "My kingdom is not of this world. If it were, my servants would fight to prevent my arrest by the Jews. But now my kingdom is from another place" (John 18:36). He came (the first time) to serve, not to be served.

So the question remains, what does it mean to be meek?

W. E. Vine, in *Vine's Expository Dictionary of Old and New Testament Words*, says that this concept of being meek is "not easily expressed in English." It refers not just to a person's outward behavior, nor just to a person's relationship with other people. It is infinitely more than a natural, human disposition. It is an internal mind-set worked into our spiritual beings by the Holy Spirit, as we yield our bodies and all personal rights to God. "Gentleness" is used to translate this Greek word in many of the newer English versions. But typically, gentleness is more appropriately related to the actions of a gentleman, while meekness is an inner condition of mind and heart. Just as we can act humbly and yet have a proud heart, and weep crocodile tears and still have a hard heart, so we can be gentle on the outside with a heart that is seething with anger on the inside.

The Greek word "praos" (meaning meekness or gentleness) is used about twenty-two times in the Bible. Christians are charged with "showing all meekness toward all men" (Titus 3:2 ASV). This inner quality of a meek and quiet spirit is very precious to God (1 Peter 3:3-4). It is a badge of honor worn by those who "live a life worthy of the calling you have received" (Ephesians 4:1-2). It is the mark of true Christian leaders (2 Timothy 2:25). This deep spiritual disposition is a characteristic of God's "elect" (Colossians 3:12). It is the foundation underneath so much of the Christian life and firmly rooted in the soil of "[counting] yourselves dead to sin but alive to God in Christ Jesus" (Romans 6:11). "You are not your own, for you were bought at a price; therefore glorify God in your body and in your spirit, which are God's" (1 Corinthians 6:19-20 NKJV).

WHAT MEEKNESS DOES NOT MEAN

Again, it is helpful to look at what this Beatitude is not in order to understand what it is. This type of introspection may be especially true of this one.

Meekness is not weakness. The concept behind this word could not be farther from the idea of weakness. You cannot be meek and weak at the same time. Contrary to our modern culture's conventional wisdom, "meekness" is a strong word. It takes a strong person to be meek. The best definition I have heard is, "Meekness is strength under control or contained." Here are some illustrations of how this word might have been used in Jesus' day. Think about shepherds around a bonfire which is controlled and contained as opposed to a wildfire out of control and causing so much damage. Think about a gentle breeze that is just the right amount of wind for sailing across the Sea of Galilee on a hot summer afternoon in contrast to a hurricane that brings death and destruction. A tamed horse still has just as much power as when it was untamed, but now it is under control. Jesus said, "I am meek" while having the power to summon 10,000 angels to deliver Him from His enemies in the garden of Gethsemane. The meek believer has more than enough power, but chooses to yield to God the right to use that power uncontrollably. Proverbs 16:32 states, "Better a patient man than a warrior, a man who controls his temper than one who takes a city." Maintaining power over your spirit is a much higher virtue than proving that you are right.

Meekness is not being deficient in courage. Dictionary definitions may lead you astray. To describe this character quality they use such words as cowardice, being flabby, and wishy-washy without any backbone. Some even suggest that it means being a sissy or effeminate. Nothing could be further from the truth. Meekness is not about being an indolent doormat.

Meekness is not a natural disposition. There are people whose personalities are more retiring than others, which does not necessarily indicate meekness. This quality is not about being a subdued person with a sense of diffidence. This is a supernatural, not natural, trait. It is part of the fruit of the Spirit (Galatians 5:22-23). Therefore, we must learn to discern the difference between the natural and supernatural.

Meekness is not polite outward mannerisms. Good manners should be one of the end-products, but meekness is much deeper. That's why I continue to use the word "meekness" rather than "gentleness." I want to be sure that we don't confuse the external activities with the internal mind-set—especially with this Beatitude. There is one place—2 Corinthians 10:1—where both "meekness" and "gentleness" are used in most English translations. There, according to Vine, the word "gentleness" denotes kindness, forbearance, clemency, not insisting on the letter of the law. Both qualities in that verse are attributed to Christ, but "meekness" seems to be the deeper of the two and is used in the passages we refer to in this chapter.

Meekness is not humility. I'm not trying to split hairs. Remember the concept of concatenation in the first chapter? That word describes two or more things coming together to become one, like two streams of water. I believe that those who use these two words interchangeably are looking downstream after they have been joined together. My position is that we get a fuller, more accurate picture when we see humility and meekness separated before they become one. In fact, all eight Beatitudes are "joined at the hip" and yet need to be seen separately, as well as after they are concatenated. Humility and meekness are obviously related. Jesus said, "I am meek and lowly [humble] in heart" (Matthew 11:29 ASV). Passages of Scripture, such as Ephesians 4:1-2 and Colossians 3:12, list these attitudes together in the same verse.

Modern culture is so preoccupied with self-assertiveness and the demanding of personal rights that it seems radical to even suggest the attitude of meekness. Think of the entire issue of entitlements that is causing so much havoc in our economy. Think of the protesters worldwide that are using demonstrations as a means of demanding their rights—and getting what they want. This demanding attitude is such a large part of our sinful nature. Who taught one-year-olds to fight over the personal ownership rights of a toy? People around us say the meek are doormats, and we know that doormats are to be stepped on. The world thinks that if you don't assert yourself, people will run over you. They say that if you don't look out for number one, who will? The overbearing win, the meek lose. So, we have all kinds of "rights movements." The magnitude of this problem is seen in our judicial system. Lawyers are inundated by people demanding their rights or making ultimatums based on their sense of entitlement. Even though it seems counterintuitive, Jesus practiced and preached something totally different. He taught that it is the meek who inherit the earth, not the survival of the fittest.

The issue here is not about right and wrong. It is about the attitude of demanding my right to demand my personal rights. Meekness does not show itself when we are wrong, but when we are right. We get a strong clue as to what this means from the word "inherit" in our text. That word means that you receive what is allotted or apportioned to you. It comes as a legacy or a gift. You receive it, you do not earn it. Jesus said "they will inherit the earth," not "they will conquer the world."

> Meekness does not show itself when we are wrong, but when we are right.

To understand the magnitude of this Beatitude, we must get down deep inside of our spiritual being. Typically, we do not receive an inheritance until someone dies. In this case, it is we who die by dying to self, to our demands, and to our right to have our own way. Furthermore, inheritance is also tied to the idea of relationship. I receive an inheritance by virtue of my relationship with the person who is granting the inheritance. We are "heirs of God and co-heirs with Christ" (Romans 8:17) because we are in Christ, and Christ is in us. This understanding brings us to the whole subject of being "crucified with Christ" (Galatians 2:20). We are to "count ourselves dead to sin, but alive to God in Christ Jesus" (Romans 6:11). Oswald Chambers wrote in *My Utmost for His Highest*, "The passion of Christianity is that I deliberately sign away my own rights and become a bond-slave of Jesus Christ." (More on this subject in the chapter entitled "The Secret for Living the Beatitudes.")

SEE MEEKNESS IN THE LIFE OF JESUS

Jesus said, "Take my yoke upon you, and learn of me; for I am meek and lowly in heart: and ye shall find rest unto your souls" (Matthew 11:29 ASV). He could make that claim because of all that we learn about Him in Philippians 2:5-11. The key idea in this passage is found in the words, "Who, being in very nature God, did not consider equality with God something to be *grasped*" [italics added] (2:6). Jesus did not demand His right to exercise His divine power while on earth as the God-Man. He didn't demand His right to be born into royalty. He didn't demand His right to a good reputation. He didn't demand His right to rule as a sovereign. He didn't demand His right to live. He didn't even demand His right to die with dignity. This is meekness personified in the mind-set of Christ. What an example!

> If I'm always defending myself, I am expressing my insecurity in God and His ability to protect me.

Throughout His time on earth, Jesus demonstrated this quality of meekness in other situations. In Pilate's hall, we see the ultimate picture. (Study passages such as Matthew 27:12-14 and 1 Peter 2:21-24.) There Christ "was led like a lamb to the slaughter, and as a sheep before her shearers is silent, so he did not open his mouth" (Isaiah 53:7). A. W. Tozer wrote a pamphlet entitled "Five Vows of Spiritual Power." One of the vows is "Never defend myself." This must be understood in the context of meekness and the example of Jesus. I am to allow my life and reputation to speak for themselves and let God and others defend me. If I'm always defending myself, I am expressing my insecurity in God and His ability to protect me.

OTHER EXAMPLES

We may be tempted to argue that since Jesus was God and we are not, we should not be expected to practice meekness as He did when He was on earth. Let's look at the example of some mere human beings. How about Abraham? He and his nephew Lot were both very wealthy men with a great many sheep and herdsmen. In Genesis 13 we read the story of their herdsmen quarreling. Abraham gave Lot the choice of which section of the land he wanted; then they would go their separate ways. As both the uncle and the older man, Abraham had the right to make that choice. Moreover, he had a covenant with God. Nevertheless, in meekness, Abraham yielded his right to choose.

Then there was Joseph who had the power, when he became prime minister of Egypt, to avenge himself against his brothers who had sold him into slavery. Now, the brothers are begging for food in the time of famine. Instead of Joseph's demanding his right for revenge, he forgave his brothers, gave them the land of Goshen as a place to live, and cared for them the remaining five years of the famine. Check out the amazing story in chapters 37 to 47 in the book of Genesis. God said, "Now the man Moses was very meek, above all the men that were upon the face of the earth" (Numbers 12:3 ASV). Jewish scholars see Moses as one of the greatest leaders in history. Interestingly, before he led the children of Israel out of Egypt, he admitted his lack of natural ability when God called him at the burning bush. Moses said to God, "Who am I to appear before Pharaoh? Who am I to lead the people of Israel out of Egypt?" (Exodus 3:11 NLT). Then God told him, "I will be with you" (Exodus 3:12 NLT). After that, Moses marched into Pharaoh's court and boldly demanded: "Let my people go!" That is strength, not weakness, on the part of the meekest man on earth.

I believe one of the reasons David was "a man after God's own heart" was his attitude of meekness. There are several stories that exhibit this quality in his life, but the one that intrigues me the most is recorded in 2 Samuel 16. Absalom, David's son, had begun a coup against his father, running his father out of town. While on the run, one of Saul's men, named Shimei, began cursing David and throwing stones at him. Abishai, David's nephew, said to David, "Let me go over and cut off his head!" (2 Samuel 16:9 NLT). As king, David had the power to do that. Instead, he yielded his right to be treated with respect saying, "Leave him alone and let him curse, for the LORD has told him to do it. And perhaps the LORD will see that I am being wronged and will bless me because of these curses" (2 Samuel 16:11-12 NLT). That is meekness at its finest.

In the New Testament we have many examples of meekness in Mary, Joseph, Stephen, and Paul. One very practical illustration is found in 1 Corinthians 9. Herein Paul makes a strong case for having personal rights—including the right to a salary so he wouldn't need to make tents for a living. Yet, he yielded those personal rights to God. He said, "I have not used any of these rights" (1 Corinthians 9:15). Paul's conclusion: "Though I am free and belong to no man, I make myself a slave to everyone, to win as many as possible" (1 Corinthians 9:19). That is meekness inside the skin of a real man.

SOME INSIGHTS REGARDING MEEKNESS AND ANGER THAT MAY BE HELPFUL

I tend to become irritated and angry when I believe that a personal right has been denied or violated. Anger has many causes. People can feel anger because others are being wronged; similar to Jesus when He cleansed the temple because people were desecrating His Father's house. However, most often anger is caused by the denial or violation of some personal right. It is a huge subject and covers a wide range of expressions. Anger comes in all shapes and sizes— from redness creeping up my neck, to passive-aggressive behavior, to rage, to murder. It can be expressed by blowing up or clamming up.

When I feel angry, the first thing I should do is identify the cause. Here is a sample checklist of personal rights we could be demanding:

- The right to life, liberty, and the pursuit of happiness
- The right to have my hopes, plans, aspirations, expectations fulfilled
- The right to have a normal standard of living
- The right to have good health and enjoy prosperity
- The right to do what I want when I want
- The right to be right
- The right to have the spiritual gift I want
- The right to have my prayers answered
- The right to get even
- The right to compare myself with others
- The right to criticize, judge, and condemn others
- The right to not suffer for righteousness' sake
- The right to be loved, accepted, understood, appreciated, supported, and cared for
- The right to date, be married, and have children
- The right to do what I want with my body
- The right to control the use of my personal belongings
- The right to privacy
- The right to be respected
- The right to express my personal opinions and idiosyncrasies
- The right to choose and to have close friends
- The right to a good education and have the job I want
- The right to be treated fairly
- The right to demand that my personal preferences be adopted by others
- The right to defend myself
- The right to have fun
- The right to go to heaven when I die

All these things may be all right. The issue is our attitude. Are we demanding our right to demand these things?

Meekness means that I yield to God whatever the right is that I am demanding and trust Him to do what is right.

It is possible to be angry and not sin (Ephesians 4:26). Not all anger is bad. Anger is an emotion. God gives us emotions to get us into motion. Someone has expressed it this way: "Blessed is the one who is always angry at the right times and in the right ways and for the right reasons and never angry at the wrong times and in the wrong ways and for the wrong reasons."

The difference is that anger which is not sinful, is anger that is under control. Someone has wisely said, "The best leader is the governor of his temper." God gets angry, but never out of control. Jesus was meek and, at the same time, cleansed the temple, without sinning. That is how Moses can be the meekest man on earth and, at the same time, break the tablets on which God had written the Ten Commandments. Remember—"meekness is strength under control." This is why it is so important to be filled with (controlled by) the Holy Spirit and experience His fruit in us, which, in part, is "self-control."

Selfish anger is typically anger that is out of control.

Experiencing (and expressing) sinful anger because some personal right has been denied or violated is a tell-tale sign that meekness is missing. Godliness with contentment is a tell-tale sign that meekness is present.

Anger-management seminars typically do not provide a permanent solution. That is like cutting off the weeds above ground rather than pulling them out by the roots.

The only solution for the problem of sinful anger is Christ's meekness in us.

Meekness includes, not excludes, responsibility. The world has turned this completely upside down. In today's society, there is strong encouragement to demand your personal rights, but there is far too little emphasis on personal responsibility. Therefore, more and more people are demanding their rights and disregarding their responsibilities. How different our world would be if we did things God's way!

Some people may think this is just a play on words. So let me use the illustration of parents disciplining their children. Suppose children do something that totally embarrasses their parents. Parents can, in out-of-control anger, discipline their children because they are demanding their right not to be embarrassed. Or parents can, under control, discipline their children because they have a responsibility to "bring them up in the training and instruction of the Lord" (Ephesians 6:4). The outcome of these two scenarios would be remarkably different.

This same principle of yielding my personal rights to God while assuming personal responsibility before God applies in so many other situations in life. We have no right to force our personal convictions on others, but we do have the responsibility to have personal convictions and consistently follow them. We have no right to expect others to give to us, but we do have a responsibility to give to others. We have no right to demand that others forgive us, but we do have the responsibility to forgive others. Husbands do not have the right to demand that their wives submit to them and respect them; husbands do have the responsibility to love and lead their wives. Wives do not have the right to demand that their husbands love them as Christ loved the church and lead them as Christ leads the church; wives do have the responsibility to submit to their husbands as unto Christ and to respect their husbands. God says we are responsible for others (i.e., I am my brother's keeper), but we do not have the right to hold others responsible for us on a personal level. It is our duty to never put a stumbling block in the way of a weaker brother (Romans 14:13), but we have no right to call ourselves weak in order to restrict the liberty of others. We are obligated to minister to others, but we have no right to demand that others minister to us. We have responsibility to pray, but we have no right to demand answers. According to the Golden Rule, we have no right to do to others as they have done to us (get even); however, we do have the responsibility to do to others as we would have them do to us.

Unexpected or unrealistic expectations are a subtle form of demanding my personal rights. Few things damage interpersonal relationships like unexpected or illegitimate expectations. David said, "My expectations are from God alone" (Psalm 62:5 KJV). This expression is just another way to convey the attitude of meekness. Such a perspective is so relevant to everyday life. For example: people give Christmas gifts to others, but when they don't get gifts in return, they stop giving. How many hidden agendas or unrealistic expectations on the part of pastors and/or congregation have ruined a local church? We must guard against both presumption and manipulation.

In leading marriage seminars I have often used the following scenarios:
"Wife: you should not expect your husband to come directly home from work every afternoon. (I quickly tell him that he had better go home or clearly explain where he will be and why.) But when he comes home, greet him warmly and let him know how glad you are that he is home. Have a good meal prepared. Create a quiet, orderly atmosphere that he enjoys when he is home. Where do you think he will go the next day after work?

Husband: don't expect your wife to have a good, home-cooked meal ready for you when you come home. When you come in the driveway and push the garage door-opener button, deliberately wind your expectations down to zero. When you walk in and smell the aroma of that good home-cooked meal, let her know how good it smells. As you eat together as a family, let her know how good it tastes. Never allow the children to speak disparagingly of her cooking. After the meal, you could even help with the dishes. What do you think she will do the next afternoon?"

Isn't this part of the same thought pattern that Peter had in mind when he wrote about wives winning their unsaved husbands to Christ? "Even if any obey not the word, they may without the word be gained by the behavior of their wives;

beholding your chaste behavior coupled with fear. Whose adorning let it not be the outward adorning of braiding the hair, and of wearing jewels of gold, or of putting on apparel; but let it be the hidden man of the heart, in the incorruptible apparel of a meek and quiet spirit, which is in the sight of God of great price (1 Peter 3:1-4 ASV).

SOME PRACTICAL SCRIPTURAL APPLICATIONS OF MEEKNESS

My attitude toward God's Word—"Receive with meekness the implanted word, which is able to save your souls" (James 1:21 ASV). We approach the Bible with a teachable spirit as life-long learners. We yield the right to any private interpretation (2 Peter 1:20). Obviously, we yield the right to take out or ignore any parts of Scripture we don't agree with or don't like. "I warn everyone who hears the words of the prophecy of this book: If anyone adds anything to them, God will add to him the plagues described in this book. And if anyone takes words away from this book of prophecy, God will take away from him his share in the tree of life and in the holy city, which are described in this book" (Revelation 22:18-19).

My attitude toward a brother who sins—"Brothers, if anyone is caught in any transgression, you who are spiritual should restore him in a spirit of gentleness [meekness]. Keep watch on yourself, lest you too be tempted" (Galatians 6:1 ESV). Typically, the old sinful nature takes delight in the fall of someone else. The rumor mills get rolling. The other person's sin makes me look better. However, God's way is to yield the right to have all those feelings and lovingly restore that person, as a doctor would reset a broken bone. Do it meekly, remembering that apart from the grace of God—there go I.

My attitude toward people who disagree with me—"Again I say, don't get involved in foolish, ignorant arguments that only start fights. A servant of the Lord must not quarrel but must be kind to everyone, be able to teach, and be patient with difficult people. Gently [meekly] instruct those who oppose the truth. Perhaps God will change those people's hearts, and they will learn the truth (2 Timothy 2:23-25 NLT). Learn to listen. Get open feedback. Never intimidate. Avoid defensiveness. Be part of the solution, not the problem.

My attitude toward comparing myself with others—"We do not dare to classify or compare ourselves with some who commend themselves. When they measure themselves by themselves and compare themselves with themselves, they are not wise" (2 Corinthians 10:12). It is not only unwise; we have no right to do it. There is an interesting scene in John 21:20-22. Jesus had just had a conversation with Peter after the resurrection, telling him the kind of death he would die. Peter turned, saw John and, thinking that John was getting a better deal, said to Jesus, "Lord, what about him?" Jesus answered, "If I want him to remain alive until I return, what is that to you? You must follow me." Since God has a unique plan for each person, what God has planned for someone else is not my business. Life may not seem fair as we think of fairness, but we are to follow the Lord.

My attitude toward division in the church—"I therefore, the prisoner in the Lord, beseech you to walk worthily of the calling wherewith ye were called, with all lowliness and meekness, with longsuffering, forbearing one another in love; giving diligence to keep the unity of the Spirit in the bond of peace. There is one body, and one Spirit, even as also ye were called in one hope of your calling" (Ephesians 4:1-4 ASV). This is a tough one. When you see something that is wrong, what do you do? I've seen two extremes: one extreme is passive silence. However, sometimes silence is not golden, it is just plain yellow. The other extreme is aggressive anger. Sometimes it includes people threatening to leave the church, if they don't get their way. (Anytime people threaten, they intuitively know their position is weak or they wouldn't even think to threaten. Leaders would do well not to cower under such threats.)

The majority of the time these quarrels come from demanding personal preferences, not biblical convictions. We need to discern the difference. The music wars in many churches are good examples. As in any art form, there are absolutes in music which should not be disregarded. On the other hand, the spirit of meekness will not permit anyone to demand that only their personal preferences in music styles are used in the worship services. That is true for people on the platform as well as in the pews. Meekness never thinks such thoughts as: I've been in this church longer than others; I've put more money in the offering plate than others; I've worked harder and longer than others, etc. Therefore, I have the right to say how things go around here. I wonder how many church splits would be avoided if everyone operated in the meekness of Christ?

My attitude toward unsaved people—"But sanctify the Lord God in your hearts, and always be ready to give a defense to everyone who asks you a reason for the hope that is in you, with meekness and fear" (1 Peter 3:15 NKJV). I suspect there is a fine line between being aggressive and taking initiative. Some are so aggressive in soul-winning that they win the argument but lose a soul. The assumption underlying this verse is that people will see something different in our lives and ask questions. That's when we need to take initiative and answer them with meekness and respect. Bottom line, we have no right to get another "notch in our belt" by praying with someone to receive Christ. We are not the soul winner, the Holy Spirit is. I believe that if He is not working in the heart of a person at the time, we can do more harm than good if we demand the right to share the gospel. In a spirit of meekness we need to be prepared for the opportunity.

IN CONCLUSION

It seems to me that there is a logical progression or a natural flow in these first three Beatitudes—which moves from humility to brokenness to meekness.

I also see such a tight concatenation, such a close connection between all three, that we could have the initial spiritual experience of all three of these Beatitudes at the same time—at least at the same kneeling before God in prayer.

But what if your initial experience of salvation was primarily a decision—maybe as a child—with very little understanding of these three Beatitudes? It would be good to study the doctrine of sin and depravity in order to understand how "poor in spirit" we really are. Study the doctrine of justification by faith to see how utterly dependent we are upon Christ as our only Savior. Come to a place of deep humility and joyful submission to the lordship of Christ in your life to experience all that it means to be under His authority.

Then, what if your conversion experience was a dry-eyed confession of sin, a mere decision of the will without the deep conviction birthed in godly sorrow for sin? It would be appropriate for you to ask the Holy Spirit for the "gift of repentance." That does not necessarily mean you were not saved at the time of your decision to receive Christ. I write this in the spirit of "Examine yourselves to see whether you are in the faith; test yourselves" (2 Corinthians 13:5). It means that you now want to experience something deeper—a godly sorrow for sin that leads to repentance. God knows how to work in our lives to bring about the mourning and weeping that result in brokenness and tenderheartedness.

> God knows how to work in our lives to bring about the mourning and weeping that result in brokenness and tenderheartedness.

But what if you still struggle with the old sin nature that manifests itself in the self-assertiveness and sinful anger that come from demanding personal rights? There is something still deeper available to us. It is a meekness that yields all possessions, personal rights, and expectations to God. It transfers the ownership of everything to God. It is totally yielding to God every part of your body as an instrument of righteousness (Romans 6:13).

This whole idea of meekness is hard for us since it requires denying self, taking up our cross, and following Christ (Matthew 16:24). It may require some major crisis to bring us to the point of totally yielding to Christ. That's what happened to Peter when he met with Jesus after the resurrection and on the day of Pentecost. Prior to the cross, he charged in where "angels fear to tread." He was the talk first/think last, sword-swinging disciple. Now look at what he writes about meekness in his epistles. That ought to give us hope. If Peter, of all people, can know the meekness of Christ, so can we.

A century ago, a song writer by the name of Elisha A. Hoffman said it this way:
> *Is your all on the altar of sacrifice laid?*
> *Your heart, does the Spirit control?*
> *You can only be blest and have peace and sweet rest,*
> *As you yield Him your body and soul.*

It is appropriate to do this now, regardless of what your previous experiences with God have been.

O God, wherever I am in my relationship with You, please show me something deeper about what it means to be truly humble before You; to weep and mourn until my heart is broken; to totally yield everything to You so I can experience and exhibit the meekness of Jesus. Amen.

PERSONAL-REFLECTION QUESTIONS
- Which personal rights do you find most difficult to yield to God?
- How are you influenced by the self-assertiveness and the demanding spirit in the world around you?
- How do you analyze your expressions (or lack of expressions) of anger?
- How have you been involved in restoring a fallen believer?

GROUP-DISCUSSION QUESTIONS
- What are some distinctions between humility and meekness?
- What can we learn from the way Jewish people expected the Messiah and relate that to our "looking for his appearing"?
- How should "My kingdom is not of this world" affect our involvement in politics?
- When should we, in a spirit of meekness, speak up, and when should we remain silent?

6

The Blessedness of Being Hungry and Thirsty for Righteousness!

Blessed are those who hunger and thirst for righteousness, for they will be filled. (Matthew 5:6)

Our great salvation is both a legal transaction and a living transmission. Seeing this big-picture concept has helped me understand so much of the Christian life. Let me begin by listing some words/phrases that convey this idea and hopefully the next few pages will explain it more fully.

LEGAL TRANSACTION—LIVING TRANSMISSION
Law—Grace
Transgressions—Guilty conscience
Christ's death—Christ's resurrection
Pardon—Forgiveness
Imputed righteousness—Imparted righteousness
Justification—Regeneration
Judicial sanctification—Experiential sanctification
Adoption—Family life
Reformation—Transformation

Biblical marriage is a beautiful object lesson that helps us understand our relationship as believers in Christ with Him as our bridegroom. Marriage is both a legal/covenant transaction and a physical/union relationship—"the two become one flesh." Our judicial system recognizes the marriage vows we make while, at the same time, the marriage relationship is also biological. Some mockingly ask, "What's the big deal about a piece of paper?" The fact is, you can have a stack of marriage licenses a mile high and still not have a biblical marriage. But having a physical union without the legal transaction is adultery or fornication, not marriage, according to the Bible. You cannot have the legal transaction without the living transmission and still call it marriage in the sight of God. Jesus said to the woman at the well, "You are right when you say you have no husband. The fact is, you have had five husbands, and the man you now have is not your husband" (John 4:17-18).

So it is with our great salvation. There is a legal transaction that includes the following theological realities:

- God declares us justified freely by His grace through faith apart from works (Romans 3:24, 28; 5:1).
- God declares that He accepts the substitutionary atonement of Christ in lieu of the death we deserve to die (Romans 3:25-26; 2 Corinthians 5:21; Hebrews 1:3; 10:12; 1 Peter 3:18).
- God legally transfers the righteousness of Christ to our record. The record of our sins is expunged (Romans 3:25; 1 John 2:2; 4:10).
- God declares that we are released from the penalty for our sins based on the ransom that Christ paid (Romans 8:1; 1 Peter 3:18).
- God officially adopts us into His family and grants to us all the legal rights as joint heirs with Christ (Galatians 4:1-7; Ephesians 1:4-5).
- God declares that we are no longer enemies now that we have been reconciled to Him by the death of His Son (Romans 5:10; 2 Corinthians 5:18).

In summary: "To all who received him [Christ], to those who believed in his name, he gave the *right* to become children of God" [italics added] (John 1:12).

The legal transactions are a once-for-all-time part of the arrangement. When the Holy Spirit brings us to the place where we acknowledge our spiritual poverty and meekly come to God with a broken and contrite spirit, God executes in heaven all the legal transactions related to our salvation in a onetime completed action. If we sin again, He does not declare us justified and impute the righteousness of Christ to our record all over again. However, "If we confess our sins, he is faithful and just and will forgive us our sins and purify us from all unrighteousness" (1 John 1:9). "For the death that He died, He died to sin once for all; but the life that He lives, He lives to God. *Likewise* you also, reckon yourselves to be dead indeed to sin, but alive to God in Christ Jesus our Lord" [italics added] (Romans 6:10-11 NKJV). Being alive in Christ is the basis for our faith in the legal transaction that God executes in heaven the moment we trust in Christ as our personal Savior.

The living transmission part includes such theological realities as the following:

- We have become partakers of the divine nature (2 Peter 1:4 ESV). God not only gave us the legal rights as His children, but we became His children. That means we were not His children before that legal transaction. It also means that we now have within us the nature of our Father which is in heaven, in contrast to the nature of "your father, the devil" (John 8:44), and your father, Adam (Romans 5:12).

- We have been born again from above (John 3:3, 7; 1 Peter 1:3, 23).
- We have been made new creatures in Christ (2 Corinthians 5:17).
- We have passed from death to life (John 5:24; Ephesians 2:1, 5; 1 John 3:14).
- We have a new heart and a new spirit (Ezekiel 36:26).

This new life in Christ is ongoing and growing from the time of our new birth until we see Christ.

As in biblical marriage, so it is in our great salvation since you cannot have a legal transaction without a living transmission. "Just as the result of one trespass was condemnation for all men, so also the result of one act of righteousness was *justification that brings life for all men*" [italics added] (Romans 5:18). If the legal transaction has happened, then the living transmission has also begun. The legal transactions are made in heaven. The living transmission happens in our hearts by the work of the Holy Spirit. We do have a reciprocal part in the legal transaction as the minor responder in the covenant arrangement. Nevertheless, God is the sovereign One who is the initiator in this covenant relationship. He also enables us to do our part by giving us the gifts of faith and repentance. (Remember, we are totally dependent upon Him for our salvation.) We do not find our assurance of salvation in the decision we make but in the promises of God and in the new life that begins to manifest itself in us. (1 John 3:4-10, 14)

On the basis of all these statements, I see the first three Beatitudes as initial requirements for entrance into the kingdom of heaven. I also see them, and the remaining Beatitudes, as the ongoing attitudes of those in whom Christ dwells by His Holy Spirit and who are, therefore, citizens in Christ's kingdom. Living all eight of the Beatitudes is evidence of a genuine conversion experience.

WHAT DOES HUNGER AND THIRST MEAN?

One of the first signs of life is hunger and thirst. This metaphor should be easy to understand. A day-old child instinctively knows about hunger and thirst. Hunger and thirst are physiological drives in us to find food and drink. This is an everyday occurrence. Food and water are necessities, not luxuries. If we don't have a good appetite, we need to see a doctor. No doubt the people on the mountainside that day knew exactly what Jesus meant when He talked about being hungry and thirsty. Some of them were more than sixty miles from home (Luke 6:17). They could have been hungry like the five thousand people that Jesus fed with five loaves and two fishes.

However, I believe the hunger and thirst that Jesus taught about that day went far beyond everyday occurrences. It is something more intense than an impulse to have a midmorning snack. It is a deep, strong, ardent, all-consuming craving for food and water. These hunger pangs are so sharp that you don't want food and a promotion at work, or food and a new car, or food and anything else. The only thought on your mind is satisfying that hunger and thirst. This concept may be difficult for Americans to grasp, since, compared with people around the world, we know very little about this kind of intense hunger and thirst.

FOR RIGHTEOUSNESS

This figure of speech takes us from the physical to spiritual hungering and thirsting and teaches us to have a passionate pursuit for righteousness. Righteousness is one of those big, all-encompassing theological words which Scripture never really defines. "God is righteousness." It is one of His compound names—"The LORD Our Righteousness" (Jeremiah 23:6). His laws are righteous. God will judge the world in righteousness. This attribute may be vague until we see Christ, the Son of God, in bodily form living the perfectly righteous life. "Christ Jesus, who has become for us . . . our righteousness" (1 Corinthians 1:30). Everything about the kingdom of heaven is righteous. Christians are to live righteously—right with God and right with others. "Righteousness exalts a nation, but sin is a disgrace to any people" (Proverbs 14:34). "Righteousness" and "unrighteousness" are words we can use as another way to describe good and evil, right and wrong, etc. "Let us hear the conclusion of the whole matter: Fear God, and keep his commandments: for this is the whole duty of man" (Ecclesiastes 12:13 KJV).

> Everything about the kingdom of heaven is righteous.

This righteousness is a pattern of inner conformity to the will of God, not about our own righteousness. Although most people think they have the right to determine what is right and wrong, God is actually the only one who has that right. He says that our righteousness is as filthy rags in his sight (Isaiah 64:6). Jesus said, "Unless your righteousness surpasses that of the Pharisees and the teachers of the law, you will certainly not enter the kingdom of heaven" (Matthew 5:20). Paul makes it clear that it is not about "having a righteousness of my own that comes from the law, but that which is through faith in Christ—the righteousness that comes from God and is by faith" (Philippians 3:4). In Romans 3:20 we read, "No one will be declared righteous in his [God's] sight by observing the law." Paul also wrote in Titus 3:5: "He saved us, not because of righteous things we had done, but because of his mercy."

Here is a simple, brief sketch of Christ's gift of righteousness to us:

Declared righteous	imputed	justification	freedom from the penalty of sin
Living righteously	imparted	sanctification	freedom from the power of sin
Perfect righteousness	eternal	glorification	freedom from the presence of sin

Therefore, it is theologically correct to say, "I have been saved" (justification), "I am being saved" (regeneration/sanctification), and "I will be saved" (glorification).

Imputed righteousness is the legal transaction part of our great salvation. God is "just and the one who justifies those who have faith in Jesus" (Romans 3:26). Abraham "believed God, and it was *credited* to him as righteousness" [italics added] (Galatians 3:6). Dr. George Guthrie of Union University writes: "Justification is a forensic act imputing the righteousness of Christ to the believer. It is not an actual infusing of holiness into the individual. It is a matter of declaring the person righteous, as a judge does in acquitting the accused." God blots out our sins and legally transfers the righteousness of Christ to our record in heaven. Our legal standing before God is just as if we had never sinned. Even better, we are legally as righteous as Christ. According to the supreme judge of the universe, the persons who come recognizing their dependence, who are broken and meek, and by faith receive Christ as their only Savior, have nothing on record in heaven for which they can be eternally condemned.

Imparted or implanted righteousness is the living transmission part of our great salvation. This means that the righteousness of God is conveyed into us by the miraculous, supernatural work of the Holy Spirit. We "participate in" (2 Peter 1:4) this progressive metamorphosis, but it is God who imparts or implants His righteousness into us. We now have a new spiritual DNA operating in us. We are alive spiritually. We have new desires, appetites, cravings, drives, and passions. The most basic of these is a hunger and thirst for God's righteousness.

The premise underneath this Beatitude is that you cannot have imputed righteousness without imparted or implanted righteousness. I may want to argue that the legal transaction takes place one nanosecond before the living transmission begins. That's because, in our finite, human logic, we cannot imagine God being just and imparting His very life to someone who is not in a right standing before Him. We also know that God does not impart His life to someone and then seeing there is something good in that person, on that basis, declare that person to be legally righteous.

Imputed righteousness is a one-time legal transaction. I am never more righteous in my standing before God than I was at that crisis point of genuine conversion. Imparted or implanted righteousness begins to operate in me at the same time as the imputed righteousness, or legal transaction, is executed. However, the new life continues to develop, grow, and mature as we hunger and thirst for righteousness. Blessed is the person who desperately longs for righteousness as a starving person longs for food and as a person who is dying of thirst longs for water. All of this—including the appetite for righteousness—is the grace of God operating in each of us, "for it is God who works in you to *will* and to *act* according to his good purpose" [italics added] (Philippians 2:13).

SEE THIS BEATITUDE IN THE LIFE OF JESUS

While examples of this behavior are not as easy to find in the life of Christ as some of the other Beatitudes, we know that this deep desire permeated His entire life on earth. Spending forty days fasting in the desert and whole nights in prayer are just two glimpses into this aspect of His life. It was His habit to be in the synagogue on Sabbath days (Luke 4:16) and He regularly prayed on the Mount of Olives (Luke 22:39). He said, "I have food to eat that you know nothing about. . . . My food . . . is to do the will of him who sent me and to finish his work" (John 4:32-34). Jesus enjoyed being with children, feasting at banquets, watching the birds fly and the lilies grow, but His most powerful craving was to conform to the will of His Father. In the garden of Gethsemane and throughout His life on earth, Jesus deeply desired to please His Father (John 5:30; 8:29). In the upper room with His disciples He said, "I have *eagerly desired* to eat this Passover with you before I suffer. For I tell you, I will not eat it again until it finds fulfillment in the kingdom of God" [italics added] (Luke 22:15-16). Jesus was and is a person with deep passion; every time we participate in a communion service, we should remember that Christ is eagerly waiting for the event called "The Marriage Supper of the Lamb" when He will eat with us.

Appetites and passions vary. Some people are more driven by their appetites than others. Some have given up in despair on ever satisfying their deep desires in life. Some have sadly discovered they can get by with very little internal motivation. They have become parasites on society and have lost their sense of self-worth. Lulled into complacency, they are content with a superficial knowledge about God, satisfied with the status quo, and not eager to improve, grow, or change in any way. Complacency, a deadly foe of all spiritual growth, is one of the most insidious tragedies of our day.

There are others who have strong ambitions which may be accompanied by high moral standards or conversely with evil intent. People have an appetite for things like fame, fortune, prestige, the approval of others, significance, beauty, security, comfort, and thrills. Apart from Christ people with these kinds of hunger and thirst are "gratifying the cravings of our sinful nature and following its desires and thoughts" (Ephesians 2:3). "Their destiny is destruction, their god is their stomach, and their glory is in their shame. Their mind is on earthly things" (Philippians 3:19). John writes, "Do not love the world or anything in the world. If anyone loves the world, the love of the Father is not in him. For everything in the world—the cravings of sinful man, the lusts of his eyes and the boasting of what he has and does—comes not from the Father but from the world. The world and its desires pass away, but the man who does the will of God lives forever" (1 John 2:15-17). It is so tragic when people hunger and thirst for wrong things and lesser things that will not satisfy.

The point of this manifesto that Jesus gave is that the only appetite that will bring complete and lasting satisfaction is the one that "[seeks] first his kingdom and his righteousness" (Matthew 6:33). All other desires are for lesser things. "The LORD detests the way of the wicked but he loves those who pursue righteousness" (Proverbs 15:9).

HOW SHOULD WE THEN THINK ABOUT OUR HUNGER AND THIRST FOR RIGHTEOUSNESS?

Dead people have no appetite. Some think that a study of the Beatitudes should begin with hungering and thirsting for righteousness since it is so essential for living the Christian life. It is essential for us to actually experience this Beatitude so we can be merciful, be pure in heart, be a peacemaker, etc. However, the Bible teaches that people outside of Christ are "dead in your transgressions and sins" (Ephesians 2:1). So, the first order of business is to be sure a person has "crossed over from death to life" (John 5:24). Telling unsaved people to "hunger and thirst for righteousness" is like telling a corpse in a casket to be hungry and thirsty.

Having an appetite is a sign of life. Physical hunger and thirst are involuntary impulses. We don't say to ourselves, "Self, be hungry now." It's a natural result of being alive. So it is with our spiritual appetite. It is part of our spiritual DNA. If we are born again, we cannot not have a spiritual hunger and thirst for righteousness—as weak and sickly as it may be at times.

This hunger and thirst is to be recurring. Those verbs in our text are in the present, continuous tense. Hunger and thirst are not designed to be permanently satisfied so we never desire to eat and drink again. Just as our physical bodies need regular nourishment from food and water to function properly, so our spirits, now made alive by the Holy Spirit, need regular spiritual nourishment to function properly. When Jesus said to the woman at the well, "Everyone who drinks this water will be thirsty again, but whoever drinks the water I give him will never thirst" (John 4:13-14), He was not saying that one drink of the water He talked about would be enough for the rest of her life. I believe He was saying that the water He gives will be so satisfying that we should not thirst again for anything else. There is a paradox in this Beatitude. We will be filled. But, just as we are filled after eating a hearty breakfast and hungry again by lunch time, so it is with our spiritual appetite.

Having an inner craving for food and water implies that we also eat and drink. This means that we take in that which is outside of us in order to sustain the life that is in us. Just sitting around the table, looking at the food, talking about how it was prepared, appreciating the fine china, is not eating and drinking. When we are hungry we want to eat. Eating is a mysterious activity. When we eat meat and potatoes, a digestive process begins which results in sustained life and energy throughout our bodies. There is this thing called metabolism. The word comes from the Greek language and means "to change" or "to transform." Metabolism is the chemical reaction in the body's cells that converts the fuel from food into physical energy to do everything from moving to thinking to growing. When we pause to ask the blessing before we eat a meal, we are not only thanking God for the food but we are asking God to bless it and transform it into strength for our bodies. In the same way we are to "eat" and "drink" by faith the righteousness which God supplies for our spiritual being. Therefore, we eat the Bread of Life and drink the Water of Life.

We are what we eat. That is what doctors tell us related to our physical being. Some may want to dispute that statement, but there can be no argument about it spiritually. This is not about developing our own righteousness. It is about receiving into our beings by faith the righteousness of God. As we "digest" His righteousness, we become what we eat.

Seeking God is synonymous with hungering and thirsting for righteousness. God is righteousness. It is a partial description of His divine nature. We cannot separate our pursuit of God from our hunger and thirst for righteousness. Jon Tomlinson, a songwriter, put it this way: "My goal is God Himself—not joy, nor peace, nor even blessing, but Himself, my God." The Psalmist said, "As the deer pants for streams of water, so my soul pants for you, O God. My soul thirsts for God, for the living God" (Psalm 42:1-2). "Your face, LORD, I will seek" (Psalm 27:8). This is about an ever-growing passion for greater intimacy with God Himself.

This appetite is to be in a category of intensity all by itself. God has said, "You will seek me and find me when you seek me with *all* your heart" [italics added] (Jeremiah 29:13). Someone has said, "You say you are hungry and are not satisfied. Perhaps God is not satisfied with your hunger." Seeking His righteousness is to be first in order of priority (Matthew 6:33). In the context of seeking the righteousness of God, Paul declared, "[This] one thing I do" (Philippians 3:9-14). J. N. Darby, a well-known churchman in the nineteenth century, once said, "When the prodigal son was hungry, he went to feed on the husks. But when he was starving, he went to his father." In a sermon on this Beatitude, Stephen Davey, the speaker on the radio program "Wisdom for the Heart," told the following story that illustrates this point:

Aristotle wrote of a time when one of his young students came to him and said, "Aristotle, you have wisdom that I so desire to have. How can I have it?"

Aristotle said, "Do you really want it?"

The young man said, "Master, I do."

Aristotle then said, "Well then, follow me."

He walked across the portico of the building, out into the courtyard, and without hesitating, waded directly into the pool of a fountain with water nearly waist-high. The young man hesitated, and then thought, Well, he said to follow him in order to find wisdom. So, gathering up his robe, he climbed over the edge and joined Aristotle.

When they were in the middle of the pool, Aristotle suddenly turned, grabbed the young man by the nape of the neck, pushed him under the water, and held him there. The youth thrashed his arms and kicked his legs, desperate to breathe.

At the last moment, Aristotle picked him up and carried him to the side of the pool.

The young disciple was coughing and sputtering in shock and rage, but Aristotle ignored it all until the young man stopped gasping. Aristotle then asked him, "When I held your head under water, what did you want more than anything?"

"Air, sir, air!" the young man cried.

His teacher then said, as he climbed out of the pool, "When you want wisdom as badly as you wanted air, you will have it.

Hunger for the Word of God. "Like newborn babies, crave pure spiritual milk [of the Word], so that by it you may grow up in your salvation, now that you have tasted that the Lord is good" (1 Peter 2:2-3). Job said, "I have treasured the words of his mouth more than my daily bread" (Job 23:12). Jeremiah said, "When your words came, I ate them; they were my joy and my heart's delight" (Jeremiah 15:16). "All Scripture is God-breathed and is useful for . . . correcting and training in righteousness" (2 Timothy 3:16). The Bible is not just a textbook to be studied academically to satisfy our curiosity and give us more information to store in our brain. Hunger and thirst for righteousness is not the same as thirst for knowledge. "Knowledge puffs up, but love builds up" (1 Corinthians 8:1).

God did not give us the Bible to make us smarter, but holier. Pastors and Bible teachers need to "feed the flock" and avoid the temptation of making intriguing information the primary appeal of the message. If people leave the meeting talking about the clever ability of the speaker and the interesting tidbits they learned, the real goal, unfortunately, has been missed.

> Hunger and thirst for righteousness is not the same as thirst for knowledge.

The word "Selah" is found seventy-one times in the Psalms and three times in the book of Habakkuk. There is some confusion about the origin of this word, but most Bible scholars that I've read seem to think it means to "pause" or "rest." The Amplified Bible translates it "pause and calmly think about that which was just sung or read." It seems to be somehow related to music. Since the Psalms were the hymnbook of the Israelites, it may simply be a musical mark denoting a pause when singers stopped singing and the musical instruments continued on so people could reflect on what was just sung. Maybe we need some "Selahs" in our worship services today?

God said to Joshua, "Do not let this Book of the Law depart from your mouth; meditate on it day and night, so that you may be careful to do everything written in it" (Joshua 1:8). The righteous man is described as one whose "delight is in the law of the LORD, and on his law he meditates day and night" (Psalm 1:2). Paul urges Timothy to "Meditate on these things; give yourself entirely to them, that your progress may be evident to all" (1 Timothy 4:15 NKJV). This kind of meditation engages the mind but also internalizes the truth of God's Word so it permeates our being and shows up in our lifestyle.

I "googled" the word *meditate* and scrolled through ten pages without finding anything about biblical meditation. All I discovered was an array of activities from a kind of daydreaming that relaxes people to Transcendental Meditation and other mystical religious practices. Here, we are writing about an in-depth study of the Bible. This may include memorizing it, hiding it in our hearts (Psalm 119:11), praying over it, spending time in reflective contemplation asking the Holy Spirit to illuminate our minds (Psalm 119:18), comparing Scripture with Scripture, applying it to our lives, and allowing it to do its powerful work in us. The net result is righteous thought patterns, which result in righteous actions, which in turn result in righteous character. Committing portions of Scripture to memory is like thinking God's thoughts after Him and understanding more of His thought patterns. I don't doubt that certain forms of meditation are good for our physical health. However, I'm sure that meditation on Scripture has a profound impact on our spiritual health.

Keep our focus on Christ who is our righteousness. "But we all, with unveiled face, beholding as in a mirror the glory of the Lord, are being transformed into the same image from glory to glory, just as by the Spirit of the Lord" (2 Corinthians 3:18 NKJV). How true it is that we become like the one we idolize. Helen H. Lemmel, a songwriter, captured this idea when she wrote:

Turn your eyes upon Jesus;
Look full in His wonderful face;
And the things of earth will grow strangely dim
In the light of His glory and grace.

Becoming like Christ is God's purpose for our lives and should be our goal in life. Christ is righteous. Therefore, if we are being "transformed into the same image from glory to glory," we will become more and more righteous. David said, "As for me, I will see your face in righteousness; I shall be satisfied when I awake in your likeness" (Psalm 17:15 NKJV).

Enjoy fellowship with people who have the same spiritual appetite. Let "iron sharpen iron." This is why the need to be involved in a small group of spiritually hungry and thirsty people fits into our quest for Christ-likeness.

Read biographies of people in previous generations who had this kind of spiritual appetite. My observation is that they had a deeper propensity toward the things of God than do most people living in today's fast-paced, texting, goal-driven, instant-news society.

Avoid anything that dulls your spiritual appetite. Remember when, as a child, you came in from playing wanting a snack? Mother would say, "No, that will spoil your appetite for dinner." Junk food does the same thing because we become satisfied with less nutritious food. Likewise, there are many things that ruin our spiritual appetite. "Each one is tempted when, by his own evil desire, he is dragged away and enticed" (James 1:14). Advertising agencies have powerful ways to lure us away from our hunger and thirst for righteousness. By God's grace we must discipline ourselves to avoid the lesser things. Never let the good take the place of the best. Remember the story of Mary and Martha (Luke 10: 38-42).

Engage in spiritual exercise. Just as physical exercise—and good old-fashioned hard work—enhance our physical appetite, so spiritual exercise increases our spiritual hunger and thirst for righteousness. "Train yourself to be godly. Physical training is good, but training for godliness is much better, promising benefits in this life and in the life to come" (1 Timothy 4:7-8 NLT). Let me just mention one "exercise" to illustrate the point. Paul writes to Philemon, "I pray that you may be active in sharing your faith, so that you will have a full understanding of every good thing we have in Christ" (Philemon 1:6). He seems to be saying there is a connection between the "exercise" of sharing your faith and the growth and development of your spiritual life.

Never be satisfied with being satisfied. Jesus said, "If anyone thirsts, let him come to Me and drink. He who believes in Me, as the Scripture has said, out of his heart will flow rivers of living water" (John 7:37-38 NKJV). "My cup overflows" (Psalm 23:5). Years ago we sang that little chorus in Sunday school—"My cup is full and running over." Our hunger and thirst should be so strong that it results in being full and overflowing so others will benefit from our appetite.

Times of unusual hunger and thirst for righteousness typically precede revival—personal and corporate. Oh, may God help us see the complacency in our own hearts and the dreadful conditions around us and create in us a deep hunger and thirst for Himself. May there be at least a remnant of people in whom this desire is so strong that it is the one thing we must have if we have nothing else. Yet we need more than personal spiritual health; our churches also desperately need revival in order to be healthy. And our nation urgently needs a gracious moving of the Holy Spirit in order to be healthy.

THEY [ALONE] WILL BE FILLED

This last part of our text is the promise of God. Just as there is a deep sense of satisfaction at the end of a delicious meal, so it is when we pursue God. We are satisfied beyond measure and want nothing else. The key is to not seek happiness or blessedness, but to "Seek first his kingdom and his righteousness, and all these things will be given to you as well" (Matthew 6:33).

This promise that we will be filled is found throughout Scripture. Psalm 107:9 says, "For he satisfies the thirsty and fills the hungry with good things." Psalm 34:10 says, "Those who seek the LORD lack no good thing." God said to Jeremiah, "My people shall be satisfied with my goodness" (Jeremiah 31:14 KJV). "For I will pour water on him who is thirsty, And floods on the dry ground; I will pour My Spirit on your descendants, And My blessing on your offspring" (Isaiah 44:3 NKJV). "Ho! Everyone who thirsts, come to the waters; and you who have no money, come, buy and eat. Yes, come; buy wine and milk without money and without price. Why do you spend money for what is not bread, and your wages for what does not satisfy? Listen carefully to Me, and eat what is good, And let your soul delight itself in abundance" (Isaiah 55:1-2 NKJV). Mary's song included this line; "He has filled the hungry with good things but has sent the rich away empty" (Luke 1:53).

Happy are the hungry. But it is not the hunger pangs that make us happy. Rather it is God who fills us with Himself. As we become increasingly satisfied with God, we become increasingly dissatisfied with sin. "Let those who love the LORD hate evil" (Psalm 97:10). For those who know Christ, the promise that "they will be filled" is an encouragement for our ongoing spiritual development! This is a sure thing. Here is ultimate fulfillment. It is found in Christ alone.

The Pursuit of God is a Christian classic written by A. W. Tozer. The first chapter is titled, "Following Hard after God," based on Psalm 63:8. It closes with the following prayer: "O God, I have tasted Thy goodness, and it has both satisfied me and made me thirsty for more. I am painfully conscious of my need of further grace. I am ashamed of my lack of desire. O God, the Triune God, I want to want Thee; I long to be filled with longing; I thirst to be made more thirsty still. Show me Thy glory, I pray Thee, so that I may know Thee indeed. Begin in mercy a new work of love within me. Say to my soul, 'Rise up, my love, my fair one, and come away.' Then give me grace to rise and follow Thee up from this misty lowland where I have wandered so long." Amen.

PERSONAL-REFLECTION QUESTIONS
- What do you really want more than anything else?
- Do you have doubts regarding the legal transaction part of your salvation? What are they? And why?
- What are some things that dull your appetite for righteousness?
- How would you rate your fellowship with others who have a deep longing for God?
- Is your cup full and running over?

GROUP-DISCUSSION QUESTIONS
- What are some theological ramifications related to the Legal Transaction and Living Transmission concept?
- Do you agree that we cannot have the Legal Transaction without the Living Transmission in the Christian life?
- What can happen in the lives of people who confuse these two aspects of our great salvation?
- What is the difference, if any, between the initial hunger pang for righteousness at conversion and the spiritual hunger pangs of a "seasoned saint"?
- How desperate are we to experience revival personally and as a group?

7

The Blessedness of Being Merciful!

Blessed are the merciful, for they will be shown mercy. (Matthew 5:7)

On October 2, 2006, a shooting occurred at an Amish one-room schoolhouse in Lancaster County, Pennsylvania. The gunman, Charles Carl Roberts IV, shot ten girls (aged 6–13), killing five, before committing suicide. The mercy and forgiving spirit shown in the response of the Amish community was widely discussed in the national media. On the day of the shooting, a grandfather of one of the murdered Amish girls was heard warning some young relatives not to hate the killer. A neighbor explained: "I don't think there's anybody here that wants to do anything but forgive and not only reach out to those who have suffered a loss in that way but to reach out to the family of the man who committed these acts." A Roberts family spokesman said an Amish neighbor comforted the Roberts family hours after the shooting and extended forgiveness to them. Some commentators criticized the quick and complete forgiveness, but "letting go of grudges" is a deeply rooted value in the Amish culture. The West Nickel Mines School was demolished the following week, leaving the site as a quiet pasture. The new school, named the New Hope School, was built at a different location and opened exactly six months after the shooting.

Being merciful is an enormous and complex subject. Mercy is another "communicable attribute" of God. It is an indispensable trait in the holy character of God as well as in godly people. True mercy is a distinctive Christian virtue. Religions of the world teach a perceived humanitarian doctrine whereby they overlook or dismiss the wrong that has been committed and then try to help people forget what happened. This kind of teaching is a counterfeit mercy. The kind of mercy that Jesus showed and taught is radically different. Jesus taught, "Be merciful, just as your Father is merciful" (Luke 6:36). We don't work up this kind of mercy in our own strength; rather, we receive God's mercy and pass it on to others. We overcome evil with good and answer malice with mercy.

Mercy was not a popular subject when Jesus was here on earth. It was considered a sign of weakness. The Romans admired justice and revenge, while the Greeks loved knowledge. The Jewish leaders were very demanding with all their legalistic rules and regulations. The philosophers of that day called mercy "a disease of the soul." Back then, an enemy was an enemy, and the best enemy was a dead one. In bold contrast, Jesus practiced and taught that mercy was a vital part of a healthy Christian life.

> **Mercy and legalism are incompatible, while mercy and justice are compatible.**

It is interesting that this Beatitude follows being "hungry and thirsty for righteousness." Righteousness is a necessary prerequisite to mercy. Mercy never nullifies righteousness. Mercy and legalism are incompatible, while mercy and justice are compatible. God's kind of mercy is unnatural for human beings. Apart from Christ, we tend to go toward one of two extremes: the first is to have a harsh, judgmental attitude of "an eye for an eye and a tooth for a tooth"; the second is demonstrated by a tolerant, sentimental clemency that excuses sin and condones the wrong. There is a fine distinction here because it is possible to have a passion for righteousness and lack compassion for those who fail to attain that standard of righteousness. It is also possible to have a pseudo-mercy that excuses sin and dilutes God's standard of righteousness.

Theologians tell us that being merciful means being moved with pity and extending relief to someone in misery. It is having compassion for people in need. It is an operative principle—not just a feeling. Mercy must be tangibly demonstrated in order to be biblical mercy. The Greek word used here for "mercy" is found again only in Hebrews 2:17. Some have said it is really untranslatable. However, the verb form of this word is found often in the New Testament. Newer translations often use the word "loving-kindness," which conveys both the motive and the action.

Those who have the spiritual gift of "showing mercy" (Romans 12:8) have an eye for seeing the practical needs of the needy and doing something about them. They are enabled by the Holy Spirit to get inside of someone else until they think and feel like that person and then do what that person needs. Mercy is a loving disposition whereby we feel the distress of others and are proactive in giving a "cup of water" in Christ's name (Mark 9:41).

The Bible is filled with references to the mercy of God. "The earth, O Lord, is full of your mercy" (Psalm 119:64 NKJV). "But the mercy of the Lord is from everlasting to everlasting on those who fear Him" (Psalm 103:17 NKJV).

"The Lord is longsuffering and abundant in mercy, forgiving iniquity and transgression; but He by no means clears the guilty" (Numbers 14:18 NKJV). After Nehemiah described the rebellion of the people, he said, "But you are God, ready to pardon, gracious and merciful, slow to anger, abundant in kindness, and did not forsake them" (Nehemiah 9:17 NKJV). "Through the Lord's mercies we are not consumed, because His compassions fail not. They are new every morning; great is Your faithfulness" (Lamentations 3:22-23 NKJV). Paul writes, "But God, who is rich in mercy, because of His great love with which He loved us, even when we were dead in trespasses, made us alive together with Christ" (Ephesians 2:4- NKJV). Lastly, James writes, "The Lord is very compassionate and merciful" (James 5:11 NKJV).

MERCY AND FORGIVENESS

Mercy and forgiveness are intrinsically joined together. "The Lord our God is merciful and forgiving, even though we have rebelled against him" (Daniel 9:9). Forgiveness is an act of mercy. It flows out of mercy just as mercy flows out of love. Love is more than mercy just as mercy is more than forgiveness. However, forgiveness seems to be the central attitude and act of mercy. Let's never forget the big picture of mercy; however, for the remainder of this chapter, our focus will be on this one aspect of mercy—forgiveness.

When someone wrongs us, the natural, default mode in the human heart is to get even. That default mechanism leads to all kinds of trouble. However, it all begins with the root of bitterness. The Bible says, "See to it that no one misses the grace of God and that no bitter root grows up to cause trouble and defile many" (Hebrews 12:15). Picture a weed growing with bitterness as its root.

So, how do we describe bitterness? Bitterness develops in us when something wrong has been done to us, and we choose to dwell on it rather than have a forgiving spirit. The offense begins to fester beneath the surface—like a diseased root in the ground. Soon, we have made a mountain out of a molehill. We begin "demanding our pound of flesh." Moreover, we think we have a right to get even when wronged and often add a little more than just getting even. But remember meekness?

Nobody has ever lived on planet earth without being wronged—not even Jesus. But that does not mean we have to be bitter. As believers in Christ, we live here as "aliens and strangers on earth" (Hebrews 11:13). We march to a different drumbeat. Yet some believers rationalize by exclaiming, "I can forgive but I can't forget." Would it shock you if I said, "The issue is not about forgetting"? I don't know where the Bible teaches that God forgets our sins. How can He when He is all-knowing? The Bible does teach, "For I [God] will forgive their wickedness and will remember their sins no more" (Hebrews 8:12). There is a vast difference between forgetting and choosing not to remember. Every time we try hard to forget something, we are remembering it. When a past offense comes up to our conscious mind from our subconscious mind, we have a choice to make. Will we continue rehearsing it, or will we choose not to dwell on it? If I were counseling someone who is struggling with this issue, I would suggest memorizing Philippians 4:8, making a list of thoughts to think about under each of those categories and then thinking about them.

Instead, for various reasons, people choose to continually review past offenses. They begin seething on the inside while the outside looks normal. This deception causes all kinds of trouble and defiles many. The bitter spirit soon grows into a serious "blame game." That leads to gathering as many people as possible on their side against the offender. Soon they begin to hold grudges resulting in being consumed day and night by the offense. They worry about letting the offender off the hook while failing to realize that they are the ones who are hooked. They become slaves to their resentment. Because it takes a lot of emotional energy to carry a grudge, depression sets in. Dr. S. I. McMillen, in his classic book *None of these Diseases*, makes this observation: "It is not what you eat, but what is eating you." Someone has said that bitterness is like drinking poison and then waiting for the other person to die. There are all kinds of self-destructive patterns that emerge from a bitter spirit.

God never made us to withstand the pressures of bitterness. All kinds of physical, mental, emotional, and spiritual problems are caused by an unforgiving spirit. Bitterness gives the other person power over your life and leads to a loss of joy. Bitter people hurt people because bitterness "defiles many." Holding grudges gives "the devil a foothold" (Ephesians 4:27). Bitterness opens the door for doubts concerning your salvation which cause turmoil in many people. We pray, "Forgive us our debts, as we forgive our debtors" (Matthew 6:12 KJV). Our Lord goes on to say, "If you do not forgive men their sins, your Father will not forgive your sins (Matthew 6:15). (Also read Matthew 18:23-35.) Bitterness has consequences.

So, what are we to do? The Bible says, "Get rid of all bitterness. . . . Be kind and compassionate to one another, forgiving each other, just as in Christ God forgave you" (Ephesians 4:31-32). "Bear with each other and forgive whatever grievances you may have against one another. Forgive as the Lord forgave you" (Colossians 3:13). "Bless those who persecute you; bless and do not curse. . . . Do not repay anyone evil for evil. . . . Do not take revenge, my friends, but leave room for God's wrath. . . . Do not be overcome by evil, but overcome evil with good" (Romans 12:14, 17, 19, 21). Later in the Sermon on the Mount, Jesus taught, "You have heard that it was said, 'Love your neighbor and hate your enemy.' But I tell you: Love your enemies and pray for those who persecute you, that you may be sons of your Father in heaven. He causes his sun to rise on the evil and the good, and sends rain on the righteous and the unrighteous" (Matthew 5:43-45).

SEE JESUS AS OUR EXAMPLE

The crowd that followed Jesus saw Him as a merciful person. This character trait is why so many cried out to Him for mercy. Justice and mercy came together in Christ at the cross. There "Mercy and truth have met together" (Psalm 85:10 NKJV). Because of what would transpire at Calvary, Jesus could say, "Neither do I condemn you; go and sin no more" (John 8:11 NKJV). From the cross He said to the one criminal, "I tell you the truth, today you will be with me in paradise" (Luke 23:43).

Based on His death and resurrection Christ forgives completely (1 John 1:9). "While we were still sinners, Christ died for us" (Romans 5:8) which means He forgives us when we do not deserve it. What's more, Jesus forgives repeatedly. "Peter came to Jesus and asked, 'Lord, how many times shall I forgive my brother when he sins against me? Up to seven times?' Jesus answered, 'I tell you, not seven times, but seventy-seven times'" (Matthew 18:21-22). If He taught that, don't you think He does it? When we understand the first three Beatitudes, we know this concept does not lead to presumptuous sinning. It teaches us to be ready to repeatedly forgive others when they sin against us.

Jesus also forgives permanently. He came as "the Lamb of God, who takes away the sin of the world!" (John 1:29) "You [God] do not stay angry forever but delight to show mercy. You will again have compassion on us; you will tread our sins underfoot and hurl all our iniquities into the depths of the sea" (Micah 7:18-19). The Lord says, "And I will forgive their wickedness, and I will never again remember their sins" (Jeremiah 31:34 NLT). He forgives eternally and will never taunt us with our sins that are cleansed by His blood. He will never allow those sins to adversely influence His relationship with us. He forgives us!

We are to follow the example of Jesus and have a forgiving spirit like His. If you are tempted to say: But Jesus is God. He can do this, but I can't. You are right, if you are thinking only about your own ability. But Christ who lives in us provides the strength for us to think and act as He did. Remember Stephen, the first Christian martyr, who "fell on his knees and cried out, 'Lord, do not hold this sin against them'"? (Acts 7:60) I wonder if he had been standing near the cross and heard Jesus say something very similar. Remember Abraham who prayed for Lot's deliverance from Sodom, even though Lot was wrong when he chose to move to Sodom? Joseph forgave his brothers in spite of all the terrible things they did to him. Moses earnestly prayed that his sister, Miriam, would be healed of leprosy, even though she had rebelled against him. Think about the many times David showed mercy to King Saul. In Jesus' parable of the Good Samaritan, the one who was an outcast showed mercy to his neighbor. We too should have the same forgiving spirit exhibited by these men.

Over fifty years ago, Dr. A. W. Tozer made this comment while preaching on the Beatitudes: "If we turned the eight Beatitudes inside out, they would reflect the thinking of the American culture." I wonder what he would say today. There is not a lot of true mercy floating around out there. Most people have a faulty view of biblical forgiveness. We need to be much more precise in our understanding and modeling of mercy.

WHAT A FORGIVING SPIRIT IS *NOT*

- It is *not* the opposite of justice. Mercy and justice are not incompatible in the mind of Christ. You cannot have truth without justice. You cannot have justice without punishment. God uses both mercy and justice as He sees best. The good news of the gospel is that the justice of God was satisfied when Christ was punished on the cross for our sins. God loved us so much that He sent His only begotten Son to bear our sins so that we might be acquitted. Forgiveness is very costly.
- It is *not* the elimination of all temporal consequences of sin. Adam and Eve were forgiven by God, but were still expelled from the garden of Eden. David was forgiven, but the child from that adulterous union died. It never pays to sin. Illustration: A son disobeys Dad by taking the family car without permission. He has an accident. He quickly and genuinely asks Dad for forgiveness. Dad lovingly forgives him. But when the bill for the repairs comes, Dad gives it to his son. The son asks, "What good did it do me to be forgiven?" Dad responds, "It restored our relationship! The necessity of paying the bill is part of the consequences, not punishment."
- It is *not* a human quality. God is the only source of this "legal mercy."
- It is *not* a human sentimentality that excuses sin and sweeps evil under the rug, thereby condoning what is wrong. Mercy is never soft on sin. In fact mercy has such an elevated view of the awfulness of sin that it means God can be merciful only because his Son paid the penalty for sin when He died on the cross for us.
- It is *not* pretending the offense never happened. It did happen, and it was wrong, and it hurt. Don't live in denial.
- It is *not* making light of the offense as a coping mechanism. Forgiveness never minimizes the offense.

- It is *not* feeling like a victim with a martyr complex thinking "What you did to me was okay, and you are free to do it again."
- It is *not* about forgetting. As stated before, there is a difference between forgetting and choosing not to remember. There is no mental eraser that magically removes these offenses from our memory. However, God does bring healing that goes beyond our ability to forget.
- It is *not* about saying "I forgive you" before being asked for forgiveness. Although there may be rare times when this action would be appropriate, it usually comes across as a self-righteous activity creating even more problems. Mercy is about having an internal attitude of a forgiving spirit that is ready to forgive when asked. However, it is not demanding the right to have the offending person ask for forgiveness. Normally, if you are "praying for those who persecute you" and "doing good to those who despitefully use you," the offender will know that you have a forgiving spirit. In addition, your own inner healing should not be dependent on having the offender ask for forgiveness. Having an attitude of a forgiving spirit is what brings healing, rather than a trite "I forgive you."
- It is *not* pardoning someone for some wrong that was done. That is a legal transaction which is the responsibility of God and those to whom He has delegated responsibility to administer the consequences for sin.
- It is *not* the same as reconciliation. While being reconciled is the desired result, we still can have a forgiving spirit even when the relationship is not restored. Reconciliation requires the participation of both parties.

WHAT A FORGIVING SPIRIT *IS*

- It begins by understanding that all sin is ultimately against God (Psalm 51:4).
- It is having the mind-set that understands that the eternal punishment for this offense has already been paid at Calvary. We don't need to seek further punishment, although appropriate retribution needs to be administered by proper authorities. That mind-set is totally different from having a spirit of retaliation.
- It is thinking about how much God has forgiven. "Blessed is he whose transgressions are forgiven, whose sins are covered" (Psalm 32:1). We owe God so much more than we will ever know. When He forgives us, how can we not be forgiving?
- It is both an emotional and a spiritual response that is ready to forgive when someone does something wrong to me.
- It transfers to God (and those to whom He has delegated it) the responsibility for temporal punishment.

- It yields to God the right to get even. "Do not take revenge, my friends, but leave room for God's wrath, for it is written: 'It is mine to avenge; I will repay' says the Lord" (Romans 12:19).
- It is being ready to say "I forgive you" regardless of the extent of the wrong actions of others and trusting God to deal with the offenders.
- It sees the hand of God in what has happened and knows that, ultimately, it will work together for good. Remember the story of Joseph?
- It intentionally chooses not to rehearse the offense nor allow a root of bitterness to grow up to trouble us.
- It comes to the place where we can have the same emotional response toward the person after the offense was committed as we had before. No more hard feelings toward that person. That is a lofty goal and typically won't happen immediately; however, having a forgiving spirit is not an event but an attitude in process. The fact is, we can have a forgiving spirit even if we don't feel like it.
- It includes looking for proactive ways to "love your enemies, bless those who curse you, do good to those who hate you, and pray for those who spitefully use you and persecute you" (Matthew 5:44 NKJV). Mark Twain once said, "Forgiveness is the fragrance that the flower leaves on the heel that crushed it."
- It is understanding that this is one of the most difficult things we will ever do in life.

THEY [ALONE] WILL BE SHOWN MERCY

This promise must be understood in the context of Scripture. It cannot be teaching some kind of Pollyanna-like idea that says, if I do good to everyone, everyone will do good to me. Look at Jesus. Nobody ever did more good than He did or had a more loving, forgiving spirit. Yet, He was killed. Nor can it be saying that forgiving others will earn us God's forgiveness. Showing mercy to others is not a condition for receiving mercy from God. It is proof that we have received it. Yet, an in-depth study of this subject reveals a deep connection between receiving mercy and then showing mercy and receiving more mercy.

We show mercy because we have received mercy. Mercy is for the undeserving. We can do nothing to earn our forgiveness—not even by forgiving someone who has wronged us. There is a sequence in the Beatitudes. When we experience the legal transaction part of the first three Beatitudes, there is a miraculous transmission of the very life of Christ into us. The first sign of that new life is a hunger and thirst for righteousness. The second sign is a forgiving spirit toward those who wrong us. Nothing proves more clearly that we have been forgiven than our readiness to forgive.

So, what does "They [alone] will be shown mercy" mean? Let's begin with a negative statement: "If you do not forgive men their sins, your Father will not forgive your sins" (Matthew 6:15). We know from this and other verses that if we do not forgive others, we will not feel forgiven. I chose these words carefully. I have made a distinction between pardon (legal) and mercy (emotional response) that I believe has a bearing on this discussion. I have no desire to give Satan ammunition as the "accuser of our brothers" (Revelation 12:10); at the same time, I have no desire to condone an unforgiving spirit. If we even begin to understand how much God has forgiven us, how can we withhold forgiveness from others? As an added incentive, this Beatitude promises that if we demonstrate a forgiving spirit because we have received the forgiveness of God by faith, then we will be shown mercy in a continuing cycle.

The problem with the unmerciful servant in the parable recorded in Matthew 18:21-35 was that he thought, given enough time, he could take care of his debt by himself. He never saw his debt as insurmountable. He didn't acknowledge his abject poverty. He didn't experience a godly sorrow that leads to repentance. All he knew was that the financial statement showed his debt was canceled. He was shown mercy, but in his heart he received no mercy. Therefore, he was unable to extend mercy to others.

> If we even begin to understand how much God has forgiven us, how can we withhold forgiveness from others?

From another perspective, Jesus taught, "Do not judge, or you too will be judged. For in the same way you judge others, you will be judged, and with the measure you use, it will be measured to you" (Matthew 7:1-2). In other words, in the same way you judge, you will be judged by others, and [I'm concluding] in the same way you forgive, you will be forgiven by others.

There is a law of "sowing and reaping." Jesus taught, "Forgive, and you will be forgiven. Give, and it will be given to you. A good measure, pressed down, shaken together and running over, will be poured into your lap. For with the measure you use, it will be measured to you" (Luke 6:37-38). We have no right to demand that others treat us the way we treat them, but typically that is what happens.

When we receive Christ into our lives, we are set free, free from the awful bondage of a bitter spirit. "The merciful man does good for his own soul" (Proverbs 11:17 NKJV). This internal benefit produces a winsome, attractive life that others admire and want to emulate. We can say with the Psalmist, "Surely goodness and mercy shall follow me all the days of my life; and I will dwell in the house of the Lord forever" (Psalm 23:6 NKJV). As we journey here below, we receive God's mercy, and our new instinct is to pass it on. When we do, Jesus promised that we would be shown mercy. We rest in that promise.

Lord, I experience Your new mercies every morning. Continue to develop in me an attitude of showing mercy to others. Help me to feel their distress and do something about it. Enable me never to allow a root of bitterness to grow up in my heart. Grant me the spiritual strength to forgive others as You have forgiven me. Amen.

PERSONAL-REFLECTION QUESTIONS

- Who is that one person most difficult for you to forgive? What should you do about it?
- Are there evidences of a bitter spirit in any area of your life?
- How would your life change if you were more intentional about having a forgiving spirit?
- Do you struggle with the thought that you are letting people off the hook if you forgive them?
- How often do you think about how God has forgiven you?

GROUP-DISCUSSION QUESTIONS

- What is the relationship between love, mercy, and forgiveness?
- How is mercy related to meekness and righteousness?
- When might it be appropriate to say "I forgive you" before being asked for forgiveness?
- How could you as a group help someone who struggles with bitterness?
- In everyday life, what is the practical difference between forgiveness and pardon?

8

The Blessedness of Being Pure in Heart!

Blessed are the pure in heart, for they will see God. (Matthew 5:8)

How pure does a person need to be in order to be "pure in heart"? Is "pure in heart" the same as "sinless perfection"? Can "your whole spirit and soul and body be kept blameless until our Lord Jesus Christ comes again" (1 Thessalonians 5:23 NLT) without your being perfect? How faultless does someone need to be in order to be perfect? In baseball there is such a thing as a perfect game. Is that the same as a no-hitter? No, because it is possible to pitch a no-hitter and still lose the game. A perfect game is when every batter that comes to the plate makes an out. But is it really a "perfect game" if the pitcher throws even one ball instead of all strikes?

This is really a most incredible statement that Jesus made early in the Sermon on the Mount. It is so vast that it covers the entire subject of biblical holiness. Yet, it pinpoints the need for purity in what the Bible calls the heart. The people who heard Jesus speak that day were taught by religious leaders that performing external rituals and "washing the outside of the cup" made them pure. Because they couldn't keep the law of Moses, they invented new superficial laws they could keep and hoped that this poor substitute satisfied the righteous demands of a holy God. In the process they externalized righteousness and formalized religion. Jesus taught the extreme opposite when He said that purity in the heart is the only way to see God. Inside every human being there is an innate desire to see God even though there is "no one who seeks God" (Romans 3:11); yet we all know that we have thoughts, attitudes, desires, and actions which are not pure. So, what does this verse mean?

WHAT DOES *PURE* MEAN?

The root word, "katharos," means to be cleansed from all impurities, purged from all contamination. When something is pure, it is free from all corruption and defilement. In a therapeutic counseling session, it is when the counselee releases deep, repressed hurts and feels "clean" again. In medical terms, the word "purgation" is used to describe the elimination of impurities. In the spiritual realm, it is the "blood of Jesus, his Son, [which] purifies us from all sin" (1 John 1:7). "He [Christ] saved us through the washing of rebirth and renewal by the Holy Spirit" (Titus 3:5).

"Pure" also means to be unmixed with anything else. Pure gold has been refined by fire which burned away all the dross. Pure grain means it has been winnowed and all chaff blown away. Pure metal has no alloys. Being pure is the opposite of being "double-minded," of trying to serve more than one master, of having a divided affection or loyalty.

It is interesting to discover that ancient Greeks also used this word to describe being free from debt, implying that these people were able to pay their bills. However, there is no way we can pay the debt we owe God. The only way we can be pure is to call out to God for His mercy that forgives our debts to Him.

Pure is one of those absolute words. We think in terms of pure, purer, and purest. But pure is pure. A company can advertise a soap that is 99.44% pure, but that means it is not pure. One drop of contaminated water in a gallon of pure water contaminates the entire gallon, rendering it impure. People instinctively know some things are pure and some things are impure. God's Word, not man-made religions, defines the difference.

Being pure or clean or unmixed is another way of describing biblical holiness. "For God did not call us to be impure, but to live a holy life" (1 Thessalonians 4:7). Holiness is an essential attribute of God. Theologians write: "Holiness is God's self-affirming purity." We have a *Holy* Bible and the blessed *Holy* Spirit. The Bible is filled with statements about the holiness of God. In both the Old and New Testaments God says, "Be holy, because I am holy" (Leviticus 11:45; 1 Peter 1:16). "Without holiness no one will see the Lord" (Hebrews 12:14). This enormous subject of holiness is summed up by Jesus in this one short sentence in the Beatitudes and must be part of our mind-set if we are in His kingdom.

WHAT DOES *HEART* MEAN?

The word "heart" is found 835 times in 775 verses in the New King James Version of the Bible, according to E-Sword. The study of the heart as used in Scripture is massive and complex. I know of no place in Scripture where this word is used to describe the pump inside our chest that moves blood throughout our body. Rather it is one designation of the nonmaterial part of a person along with soul, spirit, conscience, mind, will, and emotion. Some people think of the heart as only the emotional part of a person. Others think of it as the focal point of passion or enthusiasm. In the first-century world the heart was considered the region of thought, intention, and moral disposition.

Peter writes about "the hidden person of the heart" (1 Peter 3:4 NKJV). To be a person you don't need a body (God the Father and the Holy Spirit do not have a body but are persons), but you do need an intellect, emotion, and will. One of the central Bible verses in this entire study is, "As he thinks in his heart, so is he" (Proverbs 23:7 NKJV). Jesus asked, "Why do you think evil in your hearts?" (Matthew 9:4 NKJV) "Jesus knew in his spirit that this was what they were thinking in their hearts" (Mark 2:8). "But Mary treasured up all these things and pondered them in her heart" (Luke 2:19). Back before the flood, the inherent problem with humankind was evident because God saw that "the wickedness of man was great in the earth, and that every intent of the thoughts of his heart was only evil continually" (Genesis 6:5 NKJV). Hebrews 4:12 states: "The word of God . . . judges the thoughts and attitudes of the heart." These verses and many more show us that the heart has the capacity to think.

The biblical heart also has a will. "Daniel purposed in his heart" (Daniel 1:8 NKJV). "Each man should give what he has decided in his heart to give" (2 Corinthians 9:7). "But God be thanked that though you were slaves of sin, yet you obeyed from the heart that form of doctrine to which you were delivered" (Romans 6:17 NKJV). Repentance involves the will. It is a choice involving a change in the way we think and must be done from the heart. Acts 8 tells the story of Simon the sorcerer who offered money to have the same power the apostles had. Peter responded to Simon, saying: "May your money perish with you, because you thought you could buy the gift of God with money! You have no part or share in this ministry, because your heart is not right before God. Repent of this wickedness and pray to the Lord. Perhaps he will forgive you for having such a thought in your heart" (Acts 8:20-22). So the heart has a will, and we can choose to obey God from the heart.

> The biblical heart also has a will.

In addition, the heart does include emotions. In fact, all of the following emotions can be found in the heart (check out the passages for yourself): joy (Psalm 4:7), desire (Psalm 20:4; 73:7; Proverbs 6:25), sorrow (Proverbs 25:20; John 16:6), troubled (Psalm 25:17; John 14:1), broken (Psalm 34:18), suffering turmoil (Psalm 38:8), pained (Psalm 55:4), wounded (Psalm 109:22), distressed (Psalm 143:4), despised (Proverbs 5:12), heaviness (Proverbs 12:25), bitterness (Proverbs 14:10), merry (Proverbs 15:13), haughty (Proverbs 18:12), hateful (Leviticus 19:17; Psalm 105:25), envious (Proverbs 23:17; James 3:14), delight (Proverbs 27:9), anguish (2 Corinthians 2:4). This is not an exhaustive list, but the point is clear—the heart (as used in Scripture) is the whole inner being of a person with intellect, emotion, and will.

In 2 Corinthians 4:16 Paul writes, "Therefore we do not lose heart. Even though our outward man is perishing, yet the inward man is being renewed day by day" (NKJV). The "inward man" is the "hidden man of the heart." It is the inner life that a person lives before God, a life that is unknown to others who can see only the outside. This idea is not teaching there are two people living inside my body. This condition is not some kind of Doctor Jekyll and Mr. Hyde personality disorder. Rather it is teaching that the real you is the "inside you" where God looks, as contrasted with your outward appearance that people see (1 Samuel 16:7).

The problem is that we can project an image on the outside that is totally foreign to the reality on the inside. Jesus strongly reprimanded the religious leaders of His day when He said, "Woe to you, scribes and Pharisees, hypocrites! For you cleanse the outside of the cup and dish, but inside they are full of extortion and self-indulgence. Blind Pharisee, first cleanse the inside of the cup and dish, that the outside of them may be clean also. Woe to you, scribes and Pharisees, hypocrites! For you are like whitewashed tombs which indeed appear beautiful outwardly, but inside are full of dead men's bones and all uncleanness. Even so you also outwardly appear righteous to men, but inside you are full of hypocrisy and lawlessness" (Matthew 23:25-28 NKJV). Peter made the same point when he wrote to wives, "Your beauty should not come from outward adornment, such as braided hair and the wearing of gold jewelry and fine clothes. Instead, it should be that of your inner self, the unfading beauty of a gentle and quiet spirit, which is of great worth in God's sight" (1 Peter 3:3-4).

It's amazing what you can learn about a person by looking on the outside. Study the posture, the walk, the appearance, the tone of voice, the set of the jaw, the countenance, the eyes, the gestures—and you can often see what could be on the inside. The problem is that we are not sure if that message is coming from the heart or if it is the result of image-management. People are becoming more and more sophisticated in projecting a persona that is different from the real person on the inside. Hollywood is good at acting the part of someone else. Remember, there is a difference between character and reputation. The difficulty is that the real person is inside where we can't see. We must learn how to discern the difference between the inward person and the outward person without becoming judgmental.

"The heart is deceitful above all things" (Jeremiah 17:9). As soon as sin entered the human experience, Adam and Eve tried to cover it up. They intuitively knew that God saw them and that they were no longer innocent. So they covered themselves with fig leaves (Genesis 3:7). Each person has many thoughts and desires that never overflow into the observing world. We don't want others to see what is on the inside. The problem is that, although we can fool all the people some of the time and we can fool some of the people all the time, we can never fool God. "God understands all hearts, and he sees you" (Proverbs 24:12 NLT). He knows the real you! For example, praying from the heart is what counts, not praying with our lips. God listens to our prayers with a stethoscope, not a loudspeaker.

Another way to see this dichotomy is to think about what people will do in front of God that they would never do in front of other people. For example, some men would never think about having an affair because of social pressure. However, they will look at pornography or "look at a woman lustfully" and commit "adultery with her in his heart" (Matthew 5:28). People can act one way in church on Sunday and be totally different at work on Monday. Jesus said, "These people honor me with their lips, but their hearts are far from me" (Matthew 15:8). God's plan is to have the outward person so transparent that people can see through the outward person to the real person on the inside.

The real you is on the inside. That's where God is looking, and it's His judgment that ultimately counts. That's why Solomon said, "Keep your heart with all diligence; for out of it are the issues of life" (Proverbs 4:23 KJV). Jesus described the way every human being is naturally when He said, "But the things that come out of the mouth come from the heart, and these make a man 'unclean.' For out of the heart come evil thoughts, murder, adultery, sexual immorality, theft, false testimony, slander. These are what make a man 'unclean'; but eating with unwashed hands does not make him 'unclean'" (Matthew 15:18-20). "For out of the overflow of the heart the mouth speaks" (Matthew 12:34). In other words, defilement comes from within. The heart is the root of the problem.

The people who heard Jesus speak that day thought they could become pure by cleaning up the outside, by observing certain religious ceremonies and by following a good code of ethics. Most people in the world today still think that the sin problem can be fixed by performing external activities such as attending church services, doing nice things for a neighbor, giving to the poor, or by practicing religious rituals. Even our cultural values place more emphasis on pure air, pure water, and pure food than on a pure heart. They insist on a "smoke-free" environment while polluting the airwaves with all kinds of evil that defile the heart. Yet, people think that if they can just curb certain external habits, they will be clean in God's sight.

However, the real issue is located inside, in the heart. The gospel of Christ provides the only remedy. There is a sense in which God has a dilemma at this point (as if that were possible). Habakkuk 1:13 states: "Your eyes are too pure to look on evil; you cannot tolerate wrong." Yet, "The LORD looks at the heart"

(1 Samuel 16:7) which is "desperately wicked" (Jeremiah 17:9 NKJV). One time, when I was a young teenager, our Sunday school teacher brought to class a piece of red-tinted glass and a small red box. When we looked at the red box through the red glass, the box looked white. What a vivid object lesson for how God looks at us. "Though your sins are like scarlet, they shall be as white as snow" (Isaiah 1:18) when covered by the blood of Christ! The substitutionary atonement [covering] of Christ is the only remedy for an impure heart. "I, even I, am he who blots out your transgressions, *for my own sake*, and remembers your sins no more" [italics added] (Isaiah 43:25).

Christianity is not a hand religion, not a foot religion, not a head religion, but a heart religion. Everything about biblical salvation starts with the heart. To begin, "The heart is deceitful above all things, And desperately wicked; Who can know it?" (Jeremiah 17:9 NKJV). That premise is true of every human being born into this world. That's why Jesus started this sermon with "Blessed are the poor in spirit." When Peter preached on the day of Pentecost, the people were "cut to the heart and said to Peter and the other apostles, 'Brothers, what shall we do?'" (Acts 2:37) The Holy Spirit's conviction is aimed directly at the impurities in the inward man.

> Christianity is not a hand religion, not a foot religion, not a head religion, but a heart religion.

Then godly sorrow brings us to the cross in genuine repentance and the blood of Jesus "purifies us from all sin" (1 John 1:7). Paul wrote, "If you confess with your mouth, 'Jesus is Lord,' and believe in your heart that God raised him from the dead, you will be saved. For it is with your heart that you believe and are justified, and it is with your mouth that you confess and are saved" (Romans 10:9-10). At that point the heart becomes the dwelling place of God. Paul writes: "I pray that out of his glorious riches he may strengthen you with power through his Spirit in your inner being, so that Christ may dwell in your hearts through faith" (Ephesians 3:16-17). Also, God has "put his Spirit in our hearts as a deposit, guaranteeing what is to come" (2 Corinthians 1:22). The Holy Spirit does His transforming work in us from the inside out. We now want to obey God from our hearts. Realizing that God desires "truth in the inner parts" (Psalm 51:6), we now want a heart that is pure. Then we can go on living close to the Lord, abiding in Him, having a "burning heart" and sensing the unusual warmth of His love and presence as did those two disciples on the road to Emmaus (Luke 24:32).

WHAT ABOUT THE CONSCIENCE?

Somewhere inside of us there is a conscience. Although the word conscience does appear in the Old Testament, the Hebrew word is usually translated heart.

For example, "David's heart smote him" (1 Samuel 24:5 KJV). The same perspective is conveyed in the New Testament: "whenever our hearts condemn us" (1 John 3:20-21). The heart and conscience are tied together in verses such as: "The goal of this command is love, which comes from a pure heart and a good conscience and a sincere faith" (1 Timothy 1:5).

"Conscience" is the translation of a Greek word meaning "to know with." This suggests a moral consciousness which compares an action with a standard. The conscience is an internal alarm system that tells us when we have violated that standard. It is intelligence with an added moral component. Conscience is to the soul what pain is to the body. It gives off a signal when something is wrong. We all know what it is to be smitten by a guilty conscience. God equipped Adam and Eve with this ability when He made them. When they sinned, God said, "The man has now become like one of us, knowing good and evil. He must not be allowed to reach out his hand and take also from the tree of life and eat, and live forever" (Genesis 3:22).

Down through history people have given evidence to having a conscience. There is an interesting illustration in the gospel of John:

> Then the scribes and Pharisees brought to Him [Jesus] a woman caught in adultery. And when they had set her in the midst, they said to Him, "Teacher, this woman was caught in adultery, in the very act. Now Moses, in the law, commanded us that such should be stoned. But what do you say?" This they said, testing Him, that they might have something of which to accuse Him. But Jesus stooped down and wrote on the ground with His finger, as though He did not hear. So when they continued asking Him, He raised Himself up and said to them, "He who is without sin among you, let him throw a stone at her first." And again He stooped down and wrote on the ground. Then those who heard it, being convicted by their conscience, went out one by one, beginning with the oldest even to the last. And Jesus was left alone, and the woman standing in the midst. When Jesus had raised Himself up and saw no one but the woman, He said to her, "Woman, where are those accusers of yours? Has no one condemned you?" She said, "No one, Lord." And Jesus said to her, "Neither do I condemn you; go and sin no more." (John 8:3-11 NKJV)

I'd like to know what Jesus wrote. I'm sure it helped to prick their conscience. Incidentally, Jesus did not condone what that woman had done, but showed her mercy because [in my opinion] He knew what was going on in her heart.

Although everyone has a conscience, not everyone has a good conscience. The Bible teaches that God has placed basic principles of His law in every person's conscience (Romans 2:14-15). However, Paul writes, "Such teachings come through hypocritical liars, whose consciences have been seared as with a hot iron" (1 Timothy 4:2). This means that a person can override this inner voice until the warning fades away and the conscience is seared, calloused, insensitive, and unresponsive—in the same way the hide of an animal scarred with a branding iron becomes numb to further pain. We ought to be alarmed if it is becoming easier to ignore our conscience. We ought to respect our conscience. If we persist in disregarding it, the result could be as serious as becoming a serial killer, pedophile, drug addict, alcoholic, etc. This awareness is why we cannot risk "letting our conscience be our guide." In order for our conscience to function properly, it must concur with the example of Christ and Scripture as the final authority. The Bible provides additional clarity when it speaks of a "defiled conscience" (1 Corinthians 8:7; Titus 1:15), a "guilty conscience" (Hebrews 10:22), and a "weak conscience" (1 Corinthians 8:7).

It is possible by the grace of God to have a good, pure, clean, clear conscience void of offense before God and man. "Paul looked straight at the Sanhedrin and said, 'My brothers, I have fulfilled my duty to God in all good conscience to this day'" (Acts 23:1). Later he said, "I myself always strive to have a conscience without offense toward God and men" (Acts 24:16 NKJV). Paul wrote, "I thank God, whom I serve with a pure conscience, as my forefathers did" (2 Timothy 1:3 NKJV). "I tell the truth in Christ, I am not lying, my conscience also bearing me witness in the Holy Spirit" (Romans 9:1 NKJV). (In the next chapter, there is more about how to have this kind of conscience.)

PURE IN HEART

Let's put these ideas together. "Pure" is being free from all impurities and defilement. "Heart" is the "inward man" that is on the inside where God looks, in contrast with the "outward man" that people see. What is in the heart is the basis for God's judgments.

If the heart is impure, unclean, and mixed, then outward actions cannot be right in the sight of God. A pure heart is the opposite of subtlety, duplicity, guile, and hypocrisy. It is not sufficient to be pure in words and outward deportment. The goal of this new life in Christ is that the inward man and the outward man want the same things. In the context of this Beatitude, *integrity* means that the outward man and the inward man are on the same page. No putting on an act. No double-mindedness. Having a *sincere* heart is a life that is unfeigned, genuine, authentic, and real on the inside and outside. "Let us draw near to God with a sincere heart in full assurance of faith, having our hearts sprinkled to cleanse us from a guilty conscience and having our bodies washed with pure water" Hebrews 10:22). Genuine *freedom* is not the right to do what I want to do, but the inner power and desire to do what I ought to do. This is freedom from the inner turmoil that most people experience. In summary: "He who has clean hands and a pure heart, who does not lift up his soul to an idol or swear by what is false. He will receive blessing from the LORD and vindication from God his Savior. Such is the generation of those who seek him, who seek your face, O God of Jacob" (Psalm 24:4-6).

So let me try to answer the questions in the opening paragraph of this chapter. First, as with each of the Beatitudes, when God pronounces a blessing we can assume that He expects us to have that attitude. He has provided atonement for our sins that satisfies His righteous demands, and in Christ, "His divine power has given us everything we need for life and godliness" (2 Peter 1:3). Second, I don't believe that "pure in heart" and "sinless perfection" are the same. A person can be blameless without being sinless. Sinless perfection is not possible in this life. "If we claim to be without sin, we deceive ourselves and the truth is not in us" (1 John 1:8). I have never met a person who believed in the "eradication of the old sin nature" who could testify to being sinlessly perfect with no possibility of ever sinning again.

> There is nothing cheap or easy about having a pure heart before God.

Therefore, I believe that if we are experiencing the first five Beatitudes and have a pure conscience before God and people, we can have a pure heart. If that sounds easy, think again. There is nothing cheap or easy about having a pure heart before God. If that sounds like it is soft on sin, you have totally missed the point. If that sounds like living a joyful life of purity and simplicity in Christ, then you got it. It is not a stagnant life of legalism but a dynamic life of spiritual growth in which we "[constantly train ourselves] to distinguish good from evil" (Hebrews 5:14). Although not sinless, we sin less and less as our "walk in the Spirit" matures. The focus must be on the heart, not on what shows on the outside. Always remember where God is looking.

This freedom from guilt also applies to those who are hung up on past sins. Remember, when we come to Christ for salvation, God covers our sins with the blood of Christ, buries them in the deepest sea, and remembers them no more. Nevertheless, people argue: Others know that I have done wrong. How can they think of me as pure in heart? The issue is not what people think but what God thinks. One of the beautiful things I've noticed in developmentally handicapped people is that when they "blow it," they are quick to say "I'm sorry" and take whatever consequences are necessary. An hour later they can go on with life as if it never happened. In the same way God wants us to live by simple child-like faith in God's promise to forgive.

THE PURITY OF JESUS, OUR EXAMPLE

Jesus lived a sinlessly perfect life. People have accused Him of sinning, but they can't prove what doesn't exist. "Christ suffered for you, leaving you an example, that you should follow in his steps. 'He committed no sin, and no deceit was found in his mouth'" (1 Peter 2:21-22). "God made him who had no sin to be sin for us, so that in him we might become the righteousness of God" (2 Corinthians 5:21). "We have one [Christ] who has been tempted in every way, just as we are—yet was without sin" (Hebrews 4:15). There is no question that Jesus was pure in heart before God and people. Thus, Christ is either the pure, sinless Son of God, or He is the greatest charlatan to ever live on planet earth.

THEY [ALONE] WILL SEE GOD

Wow! What a promise! There are at least four ways to think about seeing God.

Seeing God with our physical eyes. But God said to Moses, "You cannot see my face, for no one may see me and live" (Exodus 33:20). "No one has seen God at any time. The only begotten Son, who is in the bosom of the Father, He has declared Him" (John 1:18 NKJV). God "alone is immortal and who lives in unapproachable light, whom no one has seen or can see" (1 Timothy 6:16). If we can't look at the sun with our physical eyes, how could we look at God?

Seeing God in our "mind's eye." We can picture things in our mind without actually seeing them. Some people can look at blueprints and visualize what the building will look like when completed. Good interior decorators have this same ability. Everybody has a mental image of God. But this way of "seeing God" is very dangerous and should be ignored.

Seeing God through the eyes of faith. "Now faith is . . . the evidence of things not seen" (Hebrews 11:1 NKJV). Even though God told Moses that he could not see Him, "by faith . . . he saw him who is invisible" (Hebrews 11:27). Peter writes: "Though you have not seen him, you love him; and even though you do not see him now, you believe in him" (1 Peter 1:8). Think of the experiences of all the people in the Bible who saw God through the eyes of faith. Job said, "I am pure and without sin; I am clean and free from guilt" (Job 33:9). That expression was similar to what God said about him in Job 1:8. Later, Job said, "My ears had heard of you but now my eyes have seen you. Therefore I despise myself and repent in dust and ashes" (Job 42:5-6). I see an upward spiral developing. We deal with sin and that clears our spiritual vision to see God. The more we see God, the more clearly we see ourselves. Isn't that what happened to Isaiah as recorded in Isaiah 6? Ezekiel wrote, "The heavens were opened and I saw visions of God" (Ezekiel 1:1). Then in Ezekiel 1:28 we read, "This was the appearance of the likeness of the glory of the LORD. When I saw it, I fell facedown, and I heard the voice of one speaking." Moses "hid his face, because he was afraid to look at God" (Exodus 3:6). What about Elijah, Daniel, Peter, Saul of Tarsus, and John the beloved disciple? Purity of heart clears the eyes of faith so that the invisible God is "visible." The more clearly and deeply we see God, the more we will live humbly, mournfully, meekly, with a hunger and thirst for righteousness, and a forgiving spirit.

Seeing God through glorified eyes. "But we know that when he appears, we shall be like him, for we shall see him as he is" (1 John 3:2). "Now we see but a poor reflection as in a mirror; then we shall see face to face" (1 Corinthians 13:12). That will be the ultimate purity and the ultimate vision of God!

WHAT IS OUR PART?

As we noted with previous Beatitudes, we are to be participating in what God is doing in our lives. The Bible does teach us to "purify [our] hearts" (James 4:8). After teaching about the second coming of Christ, John writes, "Everyone who has this hope in him purifies himself, just as he is pure" (1 John 3:3). God lives in us to enable us to become holy, a process requiring our cooperation. Our spiritual vision is blurred when the heart is not pure. The eyes of our understanding are opened when we have eyes focused on only one purpose—the glory of God (Matthew 6:22).

So what are some things we can and should do to cooperate with God in this work of purifying us?
- Confess all known sin—1 John 1:7-9.
- Hide God's Word in our hearts—Psalm 119:11; John 15:3.
- Pray like David—Psalm 51:10.
- Make no provision for the flesh (outward man)—Romans 13:14.
- Let the fire of God burn away all the dross—Isaiah 1:25; 1 Peter 1:7.
- Make a covenant with our eyes—Job 31:1.
- Keep looking to Jesus—2 Corinthians 3:18; Hebrews 12:2.
- Always remember that God looks on the heart—1 Samuel 16:7.

Let's ask David, a man after God's own heart, to lead us in the closing prayer for this chapter: "Create in me a pure heart, O God, and renew a steadfast spirit within me. . . . Search me, O God, and know my heart; test me and know my anxious thoughts. See if there is any offensive way in me, and lead me in the way everlasting. . . . May the words of my mouth and the meditation of my heart be pleasing in your sight, O LORD, my Rock and my Redeemer" (Psalms 51:10; 139:23-24; 19:14). Amen.

PERSONAL-REFLECTION QUESTIONS

- What does being pure in heart mean to you in practical everyday life?
- What do you think the "real you inside of you" looks like? Why?
- How would you evaluate the way your conscience is working?
- How have you seen God?
- How are you doing with the list of ways we can cooperate with God?

GROUP-DISCUSSION QUESTIONS

- Is pure in heart the same as sinless perfection?
- How do all the Beatitudes relate to biblical holiness?
- What new insight did you gain regarding the heart?
- How would you answer the author's questions in the first paragraph?
- What does it mean to see God?

9

The Blessedness of Being a Peacemaker!

Blessed are the peacemakers, for they will be called sons of God. (Matthew 5:9)

Try to imagine a group of terrorist leaders in a room strategizing how to spread their ideology around the world. How would you describe the atmosphere in the room? What is the mind-set behind the words spoken and the plans made? Then imagine a room filled with evangelists and missionaries who have a passion to spread the "gospel of peace" to every person in the world. How would you describe the difference? In these two scenes we have the extreme opposite poles in a spectrum that includes all degrees of peacemaking and troublemaking.

Peace is another big-picture concept. (That's part of the reason why I still believe that we can outline all that the Bible teaches about what we are to be under these eight Beatitudes.) God is the "God of peace." (See Romans 15:33; 16:20; 2 Corinthians 13:11; Philippians 4:9; 1 Thessalonians 5:23; Hebrews 13:20.) "God is not a God of disorder but of peace" (1 Corinthians 14:33). It was prophesied that Jesus would be "the Prince of Peace" (Isaiah 9:6). His birth was announced by angels who sang, "Glory to God in the highest, and on earth peace to men on whom his favor rests" (Luke 2:14). The Holy Spirit is the Spirit of peace (Romans 8:6; 14:17; Galatians 5:22). Paul writes, "The mind controlled by the Spirit is life and peace" (Romans 8:6). "The kingdom of God is not a matter of eating and drinking, but of righteousness, peace and joy in the Holy Spirit" (Romans 14:17). The Bible is a book about peace and places a high priority on making peace. The word "peace" is found 523 times in a multi-version concordance of the Bible. It is found in every New Testament book except for 1 John. This biblical peace is an essential Christian attitude and activity.

Peace is a beautiful word, full of rich meaning. It is a picture-word that conveys the idea of tranquility as experienced in a sailboat on a calm sea. It is musical harmony in which all the notes and chords blend in perfect agreement as in a symphony. It is a picture of the absence of strife as when two people walk hand in hand down a path together in one accord. When Jewish people greet someone with the word "Shalom," they are saying, "Peace to you. . . . May your life be filled with health, prosperity, and victory. . . . May you enjoy the tranquility that God brings. . . . I hope you have the highest good coming your way. . . . May you have all the righteousness, goodness, and peace that God can give." This desire for peace is one of the deepest longings in the heart of human beings.

The biblical concept of peace is much larger than the poetic mental pictures we have of peace. It has to do with a state of harmony, tranquility, and unity among people. It means to be whole or to have an inner sense of balance and quietness even when everything around is chaotic. It is much more than the absence of civil disturbance; it is deep and lasting serenity. Our English word "peace" comes from the Latin word "pax" meaning a pact or treaty between two or more people that includes an agreement on maintaining proper behavior.

PEACE WITH GOD

"'But there is no peace for the wicked,' says the LORD" (Isaiah 48:22; 57:21 NLT). "The way of peace they do not know" (Romans 3:17). Our basic problem is not a lack of peace among people; it is our lack of peace with God. The Bible tells us how peace was lost and how it can be found. "Therefore, since we have been justified through faith, we have peace with God through our Lord Jesus Christ" (Romans 5:1). Before being justified by faith, we were "God's enemies" (Romans 5:10a) and needed to be reconciled to God. We can only be "reconciled to him through the death of his Son" (Romans 5:10b). There is no other way. "For there is one God and one mediator between God and men, the man Christ Jesus, who gave himself as a ransom for all men" (1 Timothy 2:5). The good news of the gospel is that the alienation and separation between God and human beings has been bridged by what Christ did at Calvary and our simple faith in His finished work on the cross. It takes two to make peace. God has done His part, and we must do ours by His enabling.

PEACE OF GOD

God alone is the source of peace. The enemy of peace is sin. God's peace is different from the world's idea of peace. People who do not have peace with God cannot have the peace of God. Jesus said, "Peace I leave with you; my peace I give you. I do not give to you as the world gives. Do not let your hearts be troubled and do not be afraid" (John 14:27). "You will keep in perfect peace all who trust in you, all whose thoughts are fixed on you!" (Isaiah 26:3 NLT) Just as Jesus calmed the storm on the Sea of Galilee, so He calms our inner turmoil. Part of the fruit of the Spirit is "peace" (Galatians 5:22). It is a supernatural peace. It is far more wonderful than the human mind can comprehend. "The peace of God, which transcends all understanding, will guard your hearts and your minds in Christ Jesus" (Philippians 4:7). This peace does not depend on outward circumstances or inward rationalizations.

Frances Ridley Havergal lived in the mid-nineteenth century. Her relatively short life was filled with difficult challenges. When she was eleven, her mother died. Shortly after that her father remarried, and the stepmother caused much deep hurt. Frances was chronically ill. Even to get out of bed was painful. During one of her most painful periods of illness, she wrote:

> Like a river glorious is God's perfect peace,
> Over all victorious in its bright increase;
> Perfect, yet it floweth fuller every day;
> Perfect, yet it groweth deeper all the way.
> Stayed upon Jehovah, hearts are fully blessed;
> Finding, as he promised, perfect peace and rest.

This kind of peace is a gift from God. It is His peace imparted to us by the Holy Spirit.

LIVE PEACEABLY WITH EVERYONE

"God has called us to live in peace" (1 Corinthians 7:15; Hebrews 12:14). Based on "peace with God" and the "peace of God," "if it is possible, as far as it depends on you, live at peace with everyone" (Romans 12:18). Obviously, I cannot do this without the enabling of God and without the cooperation of the other person or persons. It takes two to make peace. I am responsible only for my own attitudes and actions—including being peaceable-minded and a peacemaker. Jesus said, "Be at peace with each other" (Mark 9:50). Paul wrote "Let us therefore make every effort to do what leads to peace" (Romans 14:19). From these verses, it is clear that we should live in peace.

THE PEACEMAKING MISSION OF CHRIST

The Son of God was sent on a long journey from heaven to earth to be a peacemaker. We who were "separate from Christ . . . and foreigners. . . . You who once were far away have been brought near through the blood of Christ. For he himself is our peace" (Ephesians 2:11-19). "For God was pleased to have all his fullness dwell in him [Christ], and through him to reconcile to himself all things, whether things on earth or things in heaven, by making peace through his blood, shed on the cross" (Colossians 1:19-20). "We also rejoice in God through our Lord Jesus Christ, through whom we have now received reconciliation" (Romans 5:11). "All this is from God, who reconciled us to himself through Christ" (2 Corinthians 5:18). Jesus is the greatest peacemaker that ever walked on the earth. He provided peace with God, and because of Him, we can have the peace of God. Furthermore, He left us a perfect example for being a peacemaker.

BLESSED ARE THE PEACEMAKERS

The Beatitudes are about attitudes which we have described as thought patterns or mind-sets that lead to character-building and actions. Being comes before doing. In previous Beatitudes, the attitude was stated and we needed to find its appropriate expression in our actions. In this Beatitude, we have the appropriate action—peacemaking—and need to find its appropriate inner thought pattern. Therefore, to describe this attitude, I am using the composite word "peaceable-minded." "Peacemakers who sow in peace raise a harvest of righteousness" (James 3:18). We "sow in peace" because we have the mind-set of peaceable-mindedness. It is the work of the Holy Spirit to change the heart and make it peaceable-minded—not divisive or full of strife and discord. Grace by its very nature turns vultures into doves. However, the complex ministry of peacemaking is far more than being a peace-loving person.

What peacemaking is *NOT*

Peacemaking is NOT the same as peacekeeping. When there is peace, we certainly need to "make every effort to keep the unity of the Spirit through the bond of peace" (Ephesians 4:3). However, peacekeeping often leads people to be accommodating; afraid of saying anything for fear that it will disturb the apparent peace. Peacemaking is not patching up a compromise and simply saying, "Peace!" when there is no peace (Ezekiel 13:10). Peacemaking implies that there is contention and someone needs to step in and make peace. It is proactive, not passive. It requires Christ-like love, gentleness, holy boldness, and "wisdom from above." Too often people substitute peacekeeping for peacemaking because they don't love enough to confront the issue; this does not result in true peace.

Peacemaking is NOT the same as working out a truce. Sometimes a truce is more dangerous than open conflict. A truce implies that the issues are not resolved; instead there is a temporary acquiescence without any change in behavior. An example: during the Vietnam war, both sides agreed to a suspension of fighting for Christmas Day. For that one day there was no shooting even though there was no real peace and the hostility still existed.

Peacemaking is NOT the same as evading the issues. I have deep respect for people who are genuinely humble and meek. They submit to authority and don't try to bully people. They don't demand personal rights. They understand that "It is to a man's honor to avoid strife, but every fool is quick to quarrel" (Proverbs 20:3). But that kind of mind-set is part of the first and third Beatitudes, not "peacemaking." I don't know anywhere in the world that humanistic pacifism has brought lasting peace. We cannot refuse to face a problem directly and expect it to go away. Biblical peace does not come by evading the issues or sweeping them under the rug. It is not about keeping our mouths shut and smoldering on the inside. We cannot pretend the problem is non-existent and call that peace. When there is peace, the issues have been dealt with and the conflict is over. To keep silent when we know we should speak up for truth will not bring lasting peace. Some see Gamaliel as a peacemaker (Acts 5:33-42). He said, "I advise you: Leave these men alone! Let them go! For if their purpose or activity is of human origin, it will fail. But if it is from God, you will not be able to stop these men; you will only find yourselves fighting against God." The hostility continued and so did the persecution. I believe if Gamaliel had stood up that day, taken off his Pharisaical robe, and declared himself to be with the apostles; he would have been a peacemaker. Instead, he watched as the apostles were flogged.

Peacemaking is NOT the same as appeasement. On the international scene, appeasement is a diplomatic policy aimed at avoiding war by making concessions to an aggressor. Christ-like peacemakers do not sacrifice biblical principles for expediency. We cannot tolerate evil for the sake of peace. The 1938 "Munich Pact" among Germany, Britain, France, and Italy prompted British Prime Minister Neville Chamberlain to announce that he had secured "peace for our time," but it actually served as a prelude to World War II. The Bible argues that peace can never be achieved apart from righteousness and justice. We cannot cover up sin by naming it something else and expect peace. On a personal level, the same principles apply. Hebrews 12:14 puts it this way: "Make every effort to live in peace with all men and to be holy." This is not about being a people pleaser or seeking "peace at any price." "The wisdom that comes from heaven is first of all pure; then peace-loving" (James 3:17). In the Beatitudes, "hunger and thirst for righteousness" and "pure in heart" come before "peacemakers." Peace apart from truth is a farce. In this context Christianity is necessarily an intolerant religion. Christians are always to be meek, full of mercy, and pure in heart, but should never compromise the truth. If appeasement were the goal, then Pilate would be a hero (Matthew 27:11-26).

What peacemaking *IS*

A peacemaker is one who seeks to bring harmony and reconciliation between those who are estranged. God hates "a man who stirs up dissension among brothers" (Proverbs 6:16-19). Yet there are people who seem to thrive on division, conflict, and unrest. That's why peacemakers are needed. We, as Christ's followers, have no biblical reason for viewing someone as an enemy. (Matthew 5:43-48.) The best way to deal with an "enemy" is to do everything in the power that God supplies to make that person a friend.

A peacemaker has a biblical concept of conflict. Conflicts are inevitable—even in churches. There are different levels of conflict and different approaches for mediation. The purpose of this book is not to provide a clinic on peacemaking. There are many good Christian counselors and peacemaking organizations available to help us in this ministry of peacemaking. I highly recommend the ministry of Jim VanYperen, *www.restoringthechurch.org*, and his book titled *Making Peace—A Guide to Overcoming Church Conflict*. It is important to know the Bible assumes there will be conflicts and that God has called us to be peacemakers. The issue is: will we deal with conflicts in a constructive or destructive way? Avoiding them and attacking the person with whom we are in conflict will result in more damage, not peace. There is a flow and progression with the Beatitudes. When a conflict arises, we are to live in all the previously studied Beatitudes and face the challenge of being a peacemaker.

A peacemaker is willing to sacrifice for peace. This is not taking the path of least resistance toward a cheap peace at any price. You may have to endure temporary trouble in order to bring about lasting peace. Making peace is not for the faint-hearted. It is not playing it safe so we don't get hurt. It is paying the price—as Jesus did—for peace. It means sacrificing selfish interests and getting involved in the chaos of conflict. It can get messy. Jesus came into our world (Philippians 2:1-11) to be a peacemaker. As followers of Christ, our attitude should be the same as His.

A peacemaker is a soul-winner. Our first, spontaneous response to this call as a peacemaker should be to help others find peace with God. Making peace involves spreading "the message God sent to the people of Israel, telling the good news of peace through Jesus Christ, who is Lord of all" (Acts 10:36). The most fundamental problem in the world is not conflict among nations or even conflict between people; it is that people are in conflict with God. God has provided a way for that conflict to be mediated through Christ. He has given us "the ministry of reconciliation" and "committed to us the message of reconciliation. We are therefore Christ's ambassadors, as though God were making his appeal through us. We implore you on Christ's behalf: Be reconciled to God" (2 Corinthians 5:18-20). Wow! What a privilege! What a responsibility! The prophet Isaiah said, "How beautiful on the mountains are the feet of those who bring good news, who proclaim peace, who bring good tidings, who proclaim salvation" (Isaiah 52:7).

A peacemaker makes peace on a personal level. When people hear the word "peacemaker," they often think first of world peace. Yet very few people have any influence on, or are in any position to do anything about, world peace. So let's get very practical. When there is a rift between someone else and me, how am I to respond? If the other person caused the rift, I am to be merciful and have a forgiving spirit. I am to be meek, which is the opposite of demanding a personal right to never be wronged by someone else. Conversely, what if I'm the one who caused the rift? What is my responsibility? Jesus said, "If you are offering your gift at the altar and there remember that your brother has something against you, leave your gift there in front of the altar. First go and be reconciled to your brother; then come and offer your gift" (Matthew 5:23-24). Here is where peacemaking really begins.

This kind of peacemaking is not our natural response. Typically, people try to cover up their sins. They think that if they try hard not to do it again, everything will be all right. Maybe if they do something nice to

> Typically, people try to cover up their sins.

the other person, that compensation will equal out everything. They compare themselves with others deciding that nobody is perfect and others are a lot worse than they are. They begin to blame the other person. He started it; she did more against me than I did against her, etc. Nevertheless, the rift remains, and now the conscience is troubled.

In the previous chapter we dealt with the subject of the conscience. But how do we maintain a clear conscience? We've all done and said things that hurt other people, whether intentionally or unintentionally. Our conscience sounds an alarm. What should we do? The best definition I've heard for a clear conscience void of offense before God and man is: "When nobody (including God) can point the finger at me and accuse me of doing something wrong that I have not made right." For me that one sentence has shed so much light on a number of passages in the Bible. I can testify from personal experience and from years of pastoral counseling—this kind of peacemaking works.

If I may, allow me to share a few principles related to asking for forgiveness that I've gleaned from my experiences.
- Be sure your confession and asking for forgiveness are genuine, from the heart.
- Put yourself in the position of the person you have wronged and feel the hurt that person felt.
- Go back to the second Beatitude and experience again the "godly sorrow that leads to repentance."

- Make a deep, intentional commitment before God to change the way you think and behave. You must decide if you want to change your behavior or only change the consequences.
- The circle of confession should be only as wide as the circle of offense. Otherwise, you may cause more problems than you solve.
- Ask the Holy Spirit to show what, when, where, and how to say what you need to say.
- Prepare what you are going to say as the prodigal son did (Luke 15:17-19).
- Be brief and to the point, but genuine and sincere. Don't try to explain what happened.
- Deal with the root problem, not just the surface issue. Otherwise, the offense will only reoccur.
- Never say, "I was wrong, but you were wrong, too." The other person may have been wrong also, but this is not the time to deal with that—unless the other person wants to.
- Don't say "If I wronged you or hurt you." You need to know before God that you were wrong. If not, then don't ask for forgiveness. If you try to confess just to keep the peace, it won't work. That is phony and results in a phony peace.
- Be prepared to have the other person laugh it off and not take you seriously. That may be a temporary response because that person's conscience is now activated. You can leave the conversation, knowing before God that you have done your part.
- Make restitution if it is required. You cannot steal $100 from a person and just say "I'm sorry."
- If forgiveness is extended, joyfully express your deep gratitude.

Right now, you may be feeling this is too hard, it is so humbling. Maybe that is part of God's design. Maybe it will reinforce your motivation not to do the same thing again, knowing that if you do, you will need to go through this same difficult, humiliating experience again. Otherwise, your conscience will continue to bother you.

A peacemaker mediates disputes. Mediation involves caring enough to confront someone in the spirit of meekness in order to bring about peace. It is not demanding the right to give someone a piece of my mind. Typically it requires doing some things to earn the right to mediate. In the family circle, in church life, in the community, in whatever sphere of influence a person has, the peacemaker steps into the turmoil to bring peace. Jesus got involved in a dispute between two brothers as recorded in Luke 12:13-21 by listening and then giving instruction. Jesus outlined steps to take when "your brother sins against you" (Matthew 18:15-17). The first step is just between the two people. If that fails to bring peace, then one or two others are to get involved in the peacemaking process. If that doesn't work, church leaders are to get involved. What the early church leaders did as recorded in Acts 6:1-7 is an excellent example of resolving church conflicts. They listened to the complaints and provided equal treatment for all widows.

When you have a dispute with another believer, Paul made it clear that you are not to go to a secular court; rather, "saints" are to serve as peacemakers (1 Corinthians 6:1-8). Read Paul's letters to pastors Timothy and Titus from the perspective of making peace. John confronted Diotrephes, "who loves to be first" (3 John 1:9-10) and ends his letter with "Peace to you" (3 John 1:14). As led by the Holy Spirit, peacemakers step into conflicted situations with the goal of making peace. This needs to be balanced by the admonition to "Make it your ambition to lead a quiet life, to mind your own business and to work with your hands, just as we told you" (1 Thessalonians 4:11). I have great admiration for and pray for government leaders who are devoted Christians and are working for genuine peace on a larger scale. This enormous subject of peace needs much more discussion than I am giving it here, but the peaceable-mindedness of Christ must permeate our lives wherever we are.

Peacemakers stand for righteousness. "Unfailing love and truth have met together. Righteousness and peace have kissed!" (Psalm 85:10 NLT). Righteousness and peace are not in opposition to each other. There is a warning in all this discussion about peace. Do not equate the absence of conflict with true peace. We cannot separate peace from righteousness. As good soldiers, we need to "fight the good fight of faith" (1 Timothy 6:12). We must "contend for the faith that was once for all entrusted to the saints" (Jude 1:3) without having a contentious attitude. Making peace that is not based on truth is merely "making nice." There are times when we need to stand up against the aggressive troublemaker while living the first six Beatitudes. Jesus, the Prince of Peace, said, "Do you think I came to bring peace on earth? No, I tell you, but division. From now on there will be five in one family divided against each other, three against two and two against three. They will be divided, father against son and son against father, mother against daughter and daughter against mother, mother-in-law against daughter-in-law and daughter-in-law against mother-in-law" (Luke 12:51-53). Does this passage contradict everything we read in the Bible about Jesus the peacemaker? No. These statements were made in the context of His warnings about a superficial kind of peace that the Pharisees taught and the Zealots wanted. Jesus always confronted sin although not always as gently as He did with the woman at the well or the woman caught in adultery. There are times when the need to speak out against what is wrong may cause temporary discord. Other times the need to speak up for someone else may mean strife and division along the way to true peace. Jesus stood up for His Father when He cleared the temple because they made God's house of prayer into a den of robbers (Mark 11:15-17). He disregarded the Pharisees' traditions and did good deeds on the Sabbath day to show that He was "Lord of the Sabbath" (Matthew 12:8). He scathingly rebuked the Pharisees and teachers of the law because their righteousness was the antithesis of His. He declared Himself to be the Son of God, but look at the trouble it caused. We need to follow His example and know which hill God wants us to die on.

Peacemakers qualify as church leaders and members in good standing. Paul writes, "I hear that when you come together as a church, there are divisions among you, and to some extent I believe it. No doubt there have to be differences among you to show which of you have God's approval" (1 Corinthians 11:18-19). Here is at least one good thing that can come from conflict. Peacemakers rise to the top as cream in the old-fashioned milk bottle. God hates "a man who stirs up dissension among brothers" (Proverbs 6:16-19). Paul writes "Now I urge you, brethren, note those who cause divisions and offenses, contrary to the doctrine which you learned, and avoid them" (Romans 16:17 NKJV). "If people are causing divisions among you, give a first and second warning. After that, have nothing more to do with them" (Titus 3:10 NLT). As we are to avoid troublemakers, so we are to approve those whom God approves as peacemakers. Look at the qualifications for church leaders in 1 Timothy 3:1-13 and Titus 1:5-9 from the perspective of making peace. A peaceable-minded attitude characterizes the people in Christ's church. Peacemaking is an activity that reveals who is approved by God and therefore should be approved by us. Making peace is a badge of honor in the kingdom of heaven.

> Peacemaking is an activity that reveals who is approved by God and therefore should be approved by us.

Praise God! The day is coming when peacemakers will no longer be needed because the Prince of Peace has come. "He will judge between the nations and will settle disputes for many peoples. They will beat their swords into plowshares and their spears into pruning hooks. Nation will not take up sword against nation, nor will they train for war anymore" (Isaiah 2:4). "For you shall go out with joy, And be led out with peace; The mountains and the hills shall break forth into singing before you, And all the trees of the field shall clap their hands. Instead of the thorn shall come up the cypress tree, And instead of the brier shall come up the myrtle tree; And it shall be to the Lord for a name, For an everlasting sign that shall not be cut off" (Isaiah 55:12-13 NKJV). These biblical passages reveal the ultimate peace!

THEY [ALONE] WILL BE CALLED SONS OF GOD

It is important to note that the Greek word used here is *huios*, our word for son, not *teknon*, our word for child. Both words are used in the New Testament to describe believers. Here the word for "son" is used to give emphasis to the honor and dignity we all have as sons of God. We reflect the character of God when we are characterized as peacemakers. Family resemblances are recognizable. You see a friend's son whom you haven't seen for some time and say, "Ah, I know whose son that is. I can tell because he bears resemblance to his father." Jesus is saying that peacemakers will be identified as sons of God because they are like their Father, the God of peace. What a mark of distinction! The God of peace has sent the Prince of peace to give us the Spirit of peace to make us peacemakers. If we make more trouble than peace, maybe it is time to "examine yourselves to see if your faith is genuine" (2 Corinthians 13:5 NLT).

Do we really grasp the great privilege of being called a son of God? Perhaps this is the most significant of all the promises associated with the Beatitudes. It is good to be promised the kingdom of heaven, comfort, inheritance, satisfaction, mercy, and the ability to see God through the eyes of faith. But to be identified as a son of God because we are exhibiting the characteristics of the God of peace is the greatest blessing of all.

Francis of Assisi (from whom the current Pope of the Roman Catholic Church has taken his name) was born in AD 1182 in the town of Assisi, Italy. He grew up in luxury; his companions were noblemen's sons. As a young man he was stricken by what some called a fatal disease. As he lay in bed one day, he had a vision of Christ. "He made a strong determination to renounce his old way of living to tread a life of purity and to dedicate his life to the service of God to people." God healed him. As he was beginning to live this new life, his friends mocked him, and he was ostracized by his family. He became known as "the little poor man of Assisi." However, people began to gather around him. The Order of Mendicant Friars was founded requiring a vow of poverty, chastity, love, and obedience. He died in the year 1228. He is best known for the prayer we use to close this chapter.

O Lord, make me an instrument of Thy Peace!
Where there is hatred, let me sow love;
Where there is injury, pardon;
Where there is discord, harmony;
Where there is doubt, faith;
Where there is despair, hope;
Where there is darkness, light, and
Where there is sorrow, joy.

O Divine Master, grant that I may not
so much seek to be consoled as to console;
to be understood as to understand; to be loved
as to love; for it is in giving that we receive;
It is in pardoning that we are pardoned;
and it is in dying that we are born to Eternal Life. Amen.

PERSONAL-REFLECTION QUESTIONS

- What does personal peace mean to you?
- What is your typical response to conflict?
- Describe the last time you took an unpopular stand for righteousness?
- Is there anyone who can point the finger at you and accuse you of doing something wrong that you never made right?
- Are you known more as a peacemaker or a peacekeeper?

GROUP-DISCUSSION QUESTIONS

- How would you describe the meeting of terrorists and the meeting of evangelists and missionaries in the first paragraph?
- How can we know if we have done everything we should to live peaceably with everyone?
- What is the difference between peacemaking and peacekeeping?
- How should peacemaking impact our evangelistic and missionary outreach?
- What did you think of the principles related to asking for forgiveness?